T0063856

TOP **10**
BEIJING

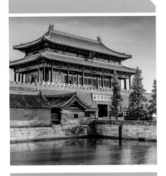

Top 10 Beijing Highlights

The Top 10 of Everything

CONTENTS

Beijing Area by Area

Streetsmart

Within each Top 10 list in this book, no hierarchy of quality or popularity is implied. All 10 are, in the editor's opinion, of roughly equal merit.

Throughout this book, floors are referred to in accordance with American usage; i.e., the "first floor" is at ground level.

Title page, front cover and spine *Colorful and intricate Chinese architecture*
Back cover, clockwise from top left *Steamed dumplings; the iconic Great Wall of China at Jinshanling; CCTV Building against the skyline of Central Business District; Chinese architecture; the impressive Temple of Heaven*

The rapid rate at which the world is changing is constantly keeping the DK Eyewitness team on our toes. While we've worked hard to ensure that this edition of Beijing is accurate and up-to-date, we know that opening hours alter, standards shift, prices fluctuate, places close and new ones pop up in their stead. So, if you notice we've got something wrong or left something out, we want to hear about it. Please get in touch at **travelguides@dk.com**

Welcome to
Beijing

From ornate temples and palaces to cutting-edge art galleries, Beijing's attractions make it a great place to explore. What was once a socialist monolith has been transformed into a cosmopolitan metropolis, with all the arts, culture, entertainment and glamor that entails. With DK Eyewitness Top 10 Beijing, it is yours to explore.

Beijing is a global city, the cultural and political hub of China. Filled with modern architecture as well as ancient sites, it has towering skyscrapers, glitzy shopping areas such as **Taikoo Li**, state-of-the-art venues for performing arts and sports, and gentrifying art districts such as **798**.

Yet amid this cosmopolitan city, lovers of antiquities still have plenty to see. The **Forbidden City** anchors the capital, and the **Summer Palace** offers respite from city noise. The conical **Temple of Heaven** graces countless guidebooks, and there are houses of worship on almost every corner – from Taoist (**White Cloud Temple**) to Buddhist (**Lama** and **Fayuan**) and Confucian to Catholic. However, the city's real charm lies in its *hutongs* – 800-year-old warrens that wind through the center – and a walk around **Hou Hai** lake, with its historical courtyard houses, offers a further glimpse of everyday life in Beijing.

Whether you're coming for a weekend or a week, our Top 10 guide brings together the best of everything that Beijing has to offer, from temple fairs to traditional crafts and tea. The guide has useful tips throughout, from seeking out what's free to places off the beaten path, plus eight easy-to-follow itineraries, designed to tie together a clutch of sights in a short space of time. Add inspiring photography and detailed maps, and you've got the essential pocket-sized travel companion. **Enjoy the book, and enjoy Beijing.**

Clockwise from top: **Great Wall of China, Temple of Heaven, the Forbidden City, Beijing's central business district, painting at the Ming Tombs, the National Stadium, Chinese lanterns**

Exploring Beijing

Beijing combines ancient history with accelerated progress, but information can be sketchy and transportation difficult, even for Chinese speakers. These two itineraries include the city's highlights and offer advice on how to make the most of your time.

Bei Hai Park is a former imperial garden. Its lake is popular for boating.

Two Days in Beijing

Day ❶
MORNING

Do some morning tai chi with the locals at the **Temple of Heaven** (see pp16–17), then browse the art stores on **Liulichang** (see p78). Stop for roast duck at **Deyuan** (see p79), then head into **Tian'an Men Square** (see pp18–19) and the **Forbidden City** (see pp12–15).

AFTERNOON

Leave by the north gate and walk to **Bei Hai Park** (see pp24–5), then over to the **Drum and Bell Towers** (see p26) for a rickshaw ride around the hutongs (traditional lanes). Enjoy a rooftop dinner at **Toast at the Orchid** (see p85), then grab a sundowner in **Hou Hai** (see pp26–7).

Day ❷
MORNING

Hire a car and driver for a trip to the **Great Wall** (see pp34–5), and make your way to Mutianyu. After hiking, grab some lunch at a local spot.

AFTERNOON

Visit the **Summer Palace** (see pp28–9). Stroll the ornate Long Corridor, climb Longevity Hill, or go boating on Kunming Lake. End the day with dinner on **Gui Jie** (Ghost Street) (see p90).

Four Days in Beijing

Day ❶
MORNING

Start off with the **Tian'an Men Square** (see pp18–19), then wander through the **Forbidden City** (see pp12–15). For lunch, dine at **Siji Minfu** (see p73), beside the Forbidden City's moat.

AFTERNOON

Take a late afternoon stroll or boat ride in **Bei Hai Park** (see pp24–5), then wander over for a walk or rickshaw ride around the hutongs of **Hou Hai** (see pp26–7). Stop at **Mr Shi's Dumplings** (see p57) for dinner before checking out cocktail bars in the streets around the Drum and Bell Towers.

Day ❷
MORNING

Join the locals in the **Temple of Heaven** (see pp16–17) for some tai

Key

— Two-day itinerary
— Four-day itinerary

chi, then head to the **Lama Temple** *(see pp20–21)* to marvel at the world's largest sandalwood Buddha. Enjoy lunch along trendy Wudaoying Hutong before browsing its boutiques and vintage stores.

AFTERNOON

Explore the maze of *hutong* lanes on either side of bustling Nanluoguxiang, with an optional pitstop at **Great Leap Brewing #6** *(see p84)* for a

The Hall of Prayer for Good Harvests can be found at **The Temple of Heaven**.

The Great Wall at Mutianyu dates from the 14th century.

glass of local craft beer. For dinner, try traditional family-style dishes at **Mr Shi's Dumplings** *(see p57)*.

Day ❸
MORNING
Get an early start and hire a private car to take you to the **Summer Palace** *(see pp28–9)*. Stop at the **Ming Tombs** *(see pp32–3)*, then carry on to the **Great Wall** *(see pp34–5)*. Enjoy a late countryside lunch at Mutianyu.
AFTERNOON
Hike to your heart's content, then sleep on a *kang* (traditional bed) in a farmer's house after a rustic dinner.

Day ❹
MORNING
Leave after breakfast and head back to the city, stopping at the **798 Art District** *(see pp30–31)*.
AFTERNOON
Grab lunch at **AT Café** *(see p31)*, and check out some of the wonderful galleries that have made Chinese contemporary art famous. Head back downtown to Sanlitun for upscale Chinese cuisine at **Jing Yaa Tang** *(see p93)*, then head over to **Migas Mercado** *(see p93)* for alfresco after-dinner drinks.

Top 10 Beijing Highlights

Colorful pavilion atop the
Forbidden City's North Gate

🔟 Beijing Highlights

At the heart of Beijing is tradition, symbolized by the Forbidden City, home to successive imperial dynasties for five centuries. Nearby, Tian'an Men Square is the China of recent times, of socialism and Mao. Beijing is also a city on the move, as a spirit of change makes it the most 21st century of capitals.

Forbidden City ①
So called because at one time only members of the imperial court were allowed inside, this is one of the largest and greatest palace complexes ever built *(see pp12–15)*.

Temple of Heaven ②

Originally the venue for annual winter solstice sacrifices, which were performed by successive emperors to ensure ample harvests, this is also one of Beijing's best spots for people-watching *(see pp16–17)*.

Tian'an Men Square ③
A politically charged icon, the world's largest city square is surrounded by cultural and political institutions. It is also the final resting place of Chairman Mao Zedong *(see pp18–19)*.

Lama Temple ④
The largest and most spectacular of the city's temples remains a working lamasery, home to monks from Mongolia and Tibet *(see pp20–21)*.

Bei Hai Park ⑤

The most beautiful of Beijing's many city parks is laid out around a central lake, first dug out in the 12th century, with the excavated earth used to create a central island. The famed Kublai Khan ruled his empire from a palace here *(see pp24–5)*.

Map labels: TUGUOLOU DAJIE · GUO HUI · Qian Hai ⑥ · DI'AN MEN WAI DAJIE · DI'AN MEN · XI DAJIE · ⑤ · Bei Hai · DIAN M · Jing Sha Park · WENJIN JIE · JING SHA QIAN JI · Zhong Hai · NANCHANG JIE · ① · Nan Hai · XI CHANG'AN JIE · ③ · QIAN MEN XI DAJI · QIAN MEN DAJIE · ZHUSHIKOU XI DAJIE · TIANQIAO NAN DAJIE

⑥ Hou Hai

By day visitors take rickshaw tours around the back lanes for a glimpse of fast-disappearing old Beijing; by night, attention shifts to the area's lake-side bars and restaurants (see pp26–7).

Around Beijing

⑩ Great Wall of China
HUAIROU
⑨ Ming Tombs
CHANGPING
SHUNYI
Summer Palace ⑦
⑧ 798 Art District
SHIJINGSHAN
TONGZHOU
Area of main map
0 km   15
0 miles   15

kilometers 1
miles 1

⑦ Summer Palace

Beijing summers are unbearably hot, so the imperial court would exchange the Forbidden City for this semi-rural retreat, with its ornate pavilions and gardens, ranged around Kunming Lake (see pp28–9).

⑧ 798 Art District

A sprawling factory complex, dating back to the 1950s, has been converted into light-filled work-shops that are home to one of Asia's best clusters of cutting-edge art galleries (see pp30–31).

⑨ Ming Tombs

Thirty miles (45 km) northwest of Beijing is the vast burial site of 13 of China's 16 Ming emperors. The most impressive sight here is the Sacred Way, with its 12 pairs of stone guardians (see pp32–3).

⑩ Great Wall of China

"Great" is something of an understatement; the Wall is nothing less than spectacular. Clamber up the perilously sloping battlements as you hike from one watchtower to another – the experience is breathtaking (see pp34–5).

⭐ Forbidden City

Officially known as the Palace Museum, this magnificent complex is a monument to the 24 emperors who ruled for a period of almost 500 years. The symbolic center of the Chinese universe, the palace was the domain of the imperial court from its completion in 1420 until the last of the emperors was forced to abdicate at the beginning of the 20th century. The modern world intruded in 1925, when sections of the palace and its treasures opened to the public for the first time. A limit of 24,000 visitors per day was introduced in 2021.

Meridian Gate 1
Known in Chinese as the *Wu Men*, this gate is the traditional entrance to the palaces. From the balcony **(right)** the emperor would review his armies and perform ceremonies marking the start of the new lunar year.

2 Hall of Supreme Harmony
Raised on a triple tier of marble terraces, this largest of halls houses a sandalwood throne **(left)**, used in the coronations of 24 emperors.

3 Inner Court
The Inner Court is more intimate than the formal Outer Court, because this is where the emperor and his consorts lived close to the emperor's concubines.

NEED TO KNOW

MAP L3 ■ North of Tian'an Men Square ■ 8500 7422 ■ Subway: Tian'an Men West or Tian'an Men East ■ en.dpm.org.cn

Open Apr–Oct: 8:30am–5pm Tue–Sun; Nov–Mar: 8:30am–4:30pm Tue–Sun

Adm Apr–Oct ¥60; Nov–Mar ¥40 (buy tickets online on www.gugong. ktmtech.cn up to 10 days in advance; passport required for entry; tickets also available on www.trip.com)

■ There are snack kiosks near the ticket office, and a restaurant inside.

■ Enter through the Meridian Gate only; other gates are for exit.

4 Imperial Garden
The emperor Qianlong wrote, "Every ruler [...] must have a garden in which he can stroll, and relax his heart." This formal garden, the oldest in the Forbidden City, has several elegant pavilions **(below)**.

7 Hall of Preserving Harmony

The most spectacular aspect of this hall **(left)** is the great carved ramp on the north side, sculpted with dragons and clouds, and made from a single piece of marble weighing more than 200 tons.

THE LAST EMPEROR

Pu Yi rose to power aged three in 1908, but he was forced to abdicate in 1912 by the new Republican government. The former emperor continued to live in the Forbidden City until 1924. Courted as a puppet ruler by the invading Japanese, he was later imprisoned by the Communists. He died in 1967, after working for seven years as a gardener.

Forbidden City

10 Gate of Supreme Harmony

The fourth and final entrance gate gives access to the Outer Court, the heart of the Forbidden City. The gate is guarded by two large bronze lions, imperial symbols of power and dignity.

5 Eastern Palaces

East of the Inner Court are smaller halls. This is where the emperor's harem lived in Qing times.

6 Western Palaces

The Palace of Gathered Elegance and the Palace of Eternal Spring, both associated with the Empress Dowager Cixi *(see p29)*, constitute the Western Palaces. Pu Yi, the last emperor, also resided in the Western Palaces.

8 Gate of Heavenly Purity

This marks the boundary between the Outer (official) and Inner Court (private) where Qing emperors would receive ministers.

9 Golden Water

Five bridges span the Golden Water **(below)**, which flows from west to east in a course designed to resemble the jade belt worn by the court officials.

🔟 Forbidden City Collections

1 Ceramics

The Hall of Martial Valor houses the Ceramics Gallery, which showcases over 1,000 priceless porcelain objects. These splendid pieces range from decorative glazed vases fired in the imperial kilns at Jingdezhen to wares used in sacrificial rituals and court weddings.

Delicately decorated ceramic vase

2 Furniture

Housed in an area known as the Southern Storehouses, the Furniture Gallery recreates Ming and Qing chambers using the palace's imperial furniture collection. After having been packed away in storerooms for decades, the lacquered tables, richly carved hardwood beds, and decorative screens were put on public display for the first time in 2018.

3 Jade

The Hall of Imperial Supremacy was built by emperor Qianlong for his retirement; it now exhibits jade artifacts. Pieces range from simple cups and ladles to enormous and intricate sculptures of Buddhas in traditional settings. The Chinese considered working this hard stone to be a metaphor for character development and the pursuit of perfection.

4 Jewelry

The Treasure Gallery in the Palace of Tranquil Longevity houses exquisite jewelry pieces. Once worn by Qing empresses and concubines, they include white jade and gemstone hairpins, thick rings, and headdresses, all adorned with all kinds of precious and semi-precious stones.

5 Beijing Opera

The Belvedere of Pleasant Sounds sports a three-story stage able to accommodate 1,000 actors. It was once rigged with trapdoors and pulleys to create dramatic entrances for supernatural characters. The exhibits include a behind-the-scenes model stage, as well as costumes, instruments, scripts, and cast lists. Screens show reconstructions of old court performances.

Ancient sundial in the Forbidden City

⑥ Musical Instruments

In true imperial fashion, the more lavish the musical entertainment, the more glory it reflected on the emperor. Court musicians used gongs of all sizes and *guqins* (zithers), wooden flutes, and heavy bronze bells adorned with dragons, as well as the unusual *sheng*, a Sherlock Holmes-style pipe with reeds of different lengths sprouting from the top. The collection is displayed in the Tower of Enhanced Righteousness, on the west side of the Outer Court.

Pagoda-topped four-sided clock

embroidered red silk decorated with ornate Chinese mythological symbols.

⑨ Clocks and Watches

Arguably the finest of all the palace treasures, the collection of clocks and watches fills the buildings south of the Hall for Ancestral Worship in the the eastern Inner Court. The creativity involved in some of the pieces, which are primarily of European origin, is astonishing. One particularly inventive model has an automaton clad in a European dress, frantically writing eight Chinese characters on a scroll, which is being unrolled by two other mechanical figures.

⑩ Empress Cixi

The Xianfu Pavilion is a memorial to the Empress Cixi's devious rise to power (see p29), as well as to the great lady's imperial extravagances, which nearly crippled her country. Clothes, jewelry, embroidered socks, imported perfume, jade and ivory chopsticks, and pictures of clothes and food form the bulk of the exhibits. There are also examples of the empress's calligraphic skills in the form of painted wall hangings.

Empress Cixi's display, Xianfu Pavilion

Bells in the instrument collection

⑦ Stone Drums

The Hall of Spiritual Cultivation holds the palace's collection of stone drums. These are enormous tom-tom shaped rocks that bear China's earliest stone inscriptions, dating back to 374 BC. These ideographic carvings, arranged in four-character poems, commemorate the glorious pastureland and successful animal husbandry that were made possible under the Emperor Xiangong's benevolent rule.

⑧ Daily Life of the Concubines

Every three years, court officials would select girls between the ages of 13 and 17 to join the eight ranks of imperial concubines. The Yonghe Pavilion exhibits clothing, games, herbal medicine, and a food distribution chart relating to the young imperial consorts, as well as the "wedding night bed," which is covered in a richly

TOP 10 ⭐ Temple of Heaven (Tian Tan)

As the Son of Heaven, the emperor could intercede with the gods on behalf of his people. Here he would pray at the winter solstice for a good harvest. Off-limits to the common people during the Ming and Qing dynasties (from the 14th to the early 20th centuries), now the temple attracts thousands of visitors daily, including many locals who come to enjoy the huge park in which the complex is set.

1 Hall of Prayer for Good Harvests

Built in 1420, then rebuilt in 1889, this circular tower, with a conical roof of blue tiles and a gold finial, is the most beautiful building in Beijing. One of the most striking facts about it is that it was constructed without the use of a single nail.

2 Painted Caisson Ceiling

The circular ceiling of the Hall of Prayer for Good Harvests has a gilded dragon and phoenix at its center **(below)**. The wood for the four central columns was imported from Oregon, as at the time China no longer had trees tall enough.

3 Temple of Heaven Park

Today, locals, inured to both the splendor of the buildings and the crowds of tourists, use the vast grounds to practice tai chi and to exercise.

4 Imperial Vault of Heaven

A circular hall made of wood and capped by a conical roof, the Imperial Vault **(above)** once held the wooden spirit tablets that were used in the ceremonies that took place on the nearby Round Altar.

5 Round Altar

The altar is formed of marble slabs laid out in nine concentric circles with each gray circle containing a multiple of nine pieces. The center of the altar represents the center of the world and it is where the emperor carried out sacrificial rites.

6 Echo Stones

There are three rectangular stones at the foot of the staircase leading up to the Imperial Vault: stand on the first and clap to hear one echo; stand on the second stone and clap once for two echoes; clap once on the third for three echoes.

Temple of Heaven (Tian Tan)

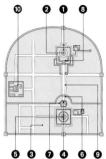

TIAN TAN

The Hall of Prayer for Good Harvests, or Qinian Dian, which is the iconic structure at the heart of the complex, is often incorrectly called the Temple of Heaven. There is, in fact, no single temple building and the name, which in Chinese is Tian Tan – a more literal translation of which is Altar of Heaven – refers to the whole complex.

Marble Platform 8

The Hall of Prayer for Good Harvests sits atop three tiers of marble that form a circle 300 ft (90 m) in diameter **(right)**. The balusters on the upper tier are decorated with carvings of dragons that signify the imperial nature of the structure.

9 Red Step Bridge

A raised walkway of marble and stone that runs along the north-south axis of the complex, the Red Step Bridge **(below)** connects the Hall of Prayer for Good Harvests with the Round Altar.

7 Echo Wall

The Imperial Vault is enclosed by the circular Echo Wall, which has the same sonic effects found in some European cathedrals, where even a whisper travels round to a listener on the other side.

NEED TO KNOW

MAP F6 ■ Tian Tan Dong Lu (East Gate), Dongcheng ■ 6702 2483 ■ Subway: Tian Tan Dong Men ■ en.tiantanpark.com

Park: open 6:30am–10pm daily; adm ¥15

Temple: open Apr–Oct: 8am–5:30pm daily (Nov–Mar: to 5pm), last entry 1.5 hrs before closing; adm ¥35, audio guides ¥40, plus deposit of ¥100

■ There are snack kiosks in the park grounds.

■ Just as fascinating as exploring the temple is observing the locals who come to the park to dance, exercise, and fly kites.

10 Hall of Abstinence

A red-walled compound surrounded by a moat spanned by bridges, this hall resembles a mini Forbidden City. This is where the emperor would spend the last 24 hours of his three-day fast prior to partaking in the Temple of Heaven ceremonies.

🔟 ⭐ Tian'an Men Square

Expanded to its current vastness in the 1950s, Tian'an Men Guangchang (Square of the Gate of Heavenly Peace) sits at the very heart of modern political China. It was here that Mao proclaimed the founding of the People's Republic, and where his embalmed body now lies. Despite the intimidating police presence, the square and its surrounding institutions are a major tourist draw.

1 **National Museum of China**

The largest museum in China **(below)** has several exhibitions which showcase the history, art and archaeological artifacts of the Chinese civilization. The artifacts date from Neolithic times to the present day.

4 **Tian'an Men**

On October 1, 1949, Mao proclaimed the founding of the People's Republic of China from this massive Ming-dynasty gate **(right)**, where his huge portrait is prominently displayed. The way to the Forbidden City is through here.

2 **Great Hall of the People**

A monolithic structure dominating the western side of the square, the Great Hall is the seat of the Chinese legislature. The vast auditorium and banqueting halls are open for part of every day except when the People's Congress is in session.

5 **Arrow Tower**

Along with the Qian Men, the Arrow Gate formed part of a great double gate. The walls that once flanked the gate were eventually demolished in the 20th century.

6 **Railway Museum**

Built by the British in 1906, one of China's first ever train stations now houses a Railway Museum. Perfect for train enthusiasts, old photos, model trains, and a full-sized replica of a modern high-speed train driver's cabin are on display.

Qian Men **3**

Also known as Zhengyang Men ("Sun-facing Gate"), the "Front Gate" **(right)** was built during the Ming dynasty. It was the largest of the nine gates of the inner city wall and it houses a city wall history museum.

7 National Flag
The Chinese flag flies at the northern end of Tian'an Men Square. People's Liberation Army (PLA) soldiers raise the flag each day at dawn and lower it back down again as the sun begins to set over the city.

9 June 4, 1989
You will not find any memorials to the 1989 pro-democracy rallies and subsequent brutal government crackdown. The event has been systematically scrubbed from Chinese memory.

CITY WALLS

It was during the Ming era (1368–1644) that the walls took on their recognizable shape of an outer wall with seven gates, and an inner wall with nine gates. Rather tragically, almost all was demolished in the 1950s and 1960s, although a small portion still stands south of Beijing Station. Today the gates are remembered in the names of the subway stations situated on the Second Ring Road.

Tian'an Men Square

8 Chairman Mao Memorial Hall
In an imposing hall at the center of Tian'an Men Square lies the embalmed body of Mao Zedong, who died in 1976. Encased in a crystal casket and draped in a red flag, the founding father of Communist China is raised from his refrigerated chamber for daily public viewings.

NEED TO KNOW

MAP L5 ■ Subway: Tian'an Men West, Tian'an Men East, or Qian Men

National Museum of China: 6511 6400; open 9am–5pm Tue–Sun (Jul & Aug: 7–11am Tue–Sun); free (passport required); en.chnmuseum.cn

Chairman Mao Memorial Hall: 6513 2277; open 8am–noon Tue–Sun; free (passport required); carrying bags, cameras, food and drinks inside, and wearing vests or sandals is prohibited

Qian Men: 6522 9384; open 9am–4.30pm Tue–Sun; adm ¥20

Railway Museum: 6705 1638; open 9am–5pm Tue–Sun; adm ¥20

Tian'an Men: 6524 3322; open 8:30am–4:30pm daily; adm ¥15

■ Entry involves security checks, so schedule plenty of time for lines.

10 Monument to the Heroes
Erected in 1958, the granite monument (below) is decorated with bas-reliefs of episodes from the nation's revolutionary history and calligraphy from Communist veterans Mao Zedong and Zhou Enlai.

TOP 10 ★ Lama Temple (Yonghe Gong)

Beijing's most spectacular place of worship is also a testament to China's long and troubled association with Tibetan Buddhism. Originally a palace for an imperial prince, it was converted to a lamasery in the 18th century and remains a functioning temple.

① Hall of the Heavenly Kings

The first of five halls, this has a plump laughing Buddha, Milefo, back-to-back with Wei Tuo, the Guardian of Buddhist Doctrine. They are flanked by the Four Heavenly Kings.

Hall of Eternal Harmony ②

This, the second hall, contains three manifestations of Buddha **(right)** representing the past, present, and future. They are flanked by 18 *luohan* – those freed from the cycle of rebirth.

④ Hall of the Wheel of Dharma

Hall four has a large statue of Tsongkhapa, the 14th-century founder of the Yellow Hat sect of Buddhism. Dominant in Tibetan politics for centuries, the sect is led by the Dalai Lama and Panchen Lama.

⑥ Hall of Ten Thousand Happinesses

The final pavilion houses a 60-ft (18-m) high Buddha carved from a single piece of sandalwood. There's a splendid collection of Tibetan Buddhist objects in the adjacent side-hall.

③ Hall of Eternal Protection

The third hall **(above)** contains Buddhas of longevity and medicine, plus two *tangkas* said to have been embroidered by Emperor Qianlong's mother. Behind the hall is a bronze sculpture of Mount Meru.

⑤ Monks

At one time there were 1,500 monks at the temple; now there are only around 70. Although of the same Yellow Hat sect as the Dalai Lama, the monks are required to reject Tibetan independence.

⑦ Prayer Wheel

Spinning a prayer wheel sends a written prayer on coiled paper to heaven. A little yellow arrow taped to the frame of the wheel reminds worshipers that the wheel is to be spun in clockwise direction.

8 Lion Statue

A large imperial lion **(left)** is a reminder that the complex was the residence of future Qing emperor Yongzheng. On ascending the throne in 1722, and in keeping with tradition, his former home became a temple.

PANCHEN LAMA

While the Dalai Lama, head of the sect to which the Lama Temple belongs, lives in exile, the second head, the Panchen Lama, resides in Beijing and recognizes Chinese authority. However, the matter of the true identity of the Panchen Lama is mired in controversy. China supports one candidate, while the Tibetans recognize another – only he was abducted, along with his family, by Chinese authorities in 1995. It is believed he is alive and living anonymously in China.

Lama Temple (Yonghe Gong)

9 Incense Burner

There are incense burners **(below)** in front of all the many altars throughout the temple. Shops lining the entryway to the complex and in the neighboring streets are piled with bundles of incense sticks for sale for use at the temple.

10 Drum and Bell Towers

The temple's Drum and Bell towers are in the first courtyard after passing through the main entrance. The huge bell **(above)** has been removed from its tower and placed on the ground.

NEED TO KNOW

MAP F1 ■ 12 Yonghe Gong Dajie ■ 6404 1919 ■ Subway: Yonghe Gong Exit C

Open 9am–4.30pm daily (Nov–Mar: to 4pm)

Adm ¥25, audio guides ¥50 (plus ¥200 deposit)

■ After visiting the temple, head to Wudaoying Hutong for its many cafés, bars, and restaurants.

■ Photography is not allowed within the halls, but you can take pictures of the exteriors and of the courtyards.

Following pages The blue-tiled Hall of Prayer for Good Harvests, Temple of Heaven

🔟 ⭐ Bei Hai Park

An imperial garden for over 1,000 years, Bei Hai was opened to the public in 1925. Filled with artificial hills, pavilions, and temples, it is associated with Kublai Khan, who redesigned it during the Mongol Yuan dynasty. These days, it is a fine place for a leisurely stroll, and a bit of boating on the lake.

① Round City

Bei Hai was the site of Beijing's earliest imperial palace, although nothing now remains other than a small pavilion on a site known as the Round City, and a huge jade wine vessel said to have belonged to Kublai Khan.

② Western Elysium

Fronted by an enormous memorial arch, this Ming-era hall on the lake's north shore is notable for its lack of paint, revealing the sumptuous quality of the cedar used in its construction.

③ Little Western Heaven

Inside this lofty hall (**left**) on the lake's north shore sits an enormous mountain diorama covered with gnome-like *arhats* (Buddhist disciples). This was a rather elaborate birthday gift from the Qianlong emperor to his mother.

④ White Dagoba

Topping Jade Island, this is a Tibetan-style stupa built to honor the visit of the fifth Dalai Lama in 1651. It has been rebuilt twice since.

PARK PLAY

Beijing's parks double as recreation centers, particularly for the city's elderly citizens. Early in the morning, they gather to perform *tai ji quan* (tai chi) exercises. Many then spend the rest of the day in the park playing cards or mahjong, engaging in *yang ge* (fan dancing) or ballroom dancing, or just reading the paper and talking with friends.

5 Jade Island
Accessed by bridge from the south gate or by boat from the north gate, Bei Hai's willow-lined island **(below)** was created from the earth excavated to form the lake.

9 Yongan Temple
Leading up to the Dagoba on Jade Island, this steep hillside temple comprises a series of ascending halls, including the Hall of the Wheel of Law, with its central effigy of the Buddha Sakyamuni **(left)**.

7 Pavilion of Calligraphy
A crescent-shaped hall on Jade Island contains nearly 500 stone tablets engraved with the work of famous Chinese calligraphers. If the exhibits are less than enthralling, the walkways that lead to the pavilion are enchanting.

8 Zhong Nan Hai
Bei Hai means "North Lake"; the Middle (Zhong) and South (Nan) Lakes were once connected but are now part of an off-limits area occupied by China's political leaders. Zhong Nan Hai is regarded as the new Forbidden City.

6 Nine Dragon Screen
This free-standing wall made of colorful glazed ceramic tiles depicts nine intertwined dragons **(above)**. The Chinese dragon is a beneficent beast offering protection and good luck. The wall was designed to obstruct the passage of evil spirits.

10 Jingxin Studio
In the northwest corner of the park **(above)** is this garden-within-a-garden, created in the mid-18th century by the Qianlong emperor, with rockeries, pavilions, and ornate bridges over goldfish-filled pools.

NEED TO KNOW

MAP K1 ■ 1 Wenjin Jie, Xicheng ■ 6403 3225 ■ info@beihaipark.com.cn ■ Subway: Beihai Bei or Tian'an Men West ■ Buses: 5, 101, 103, 107, 109, 111

Open 6:30am–9pm daily (Nov–Mar: to 8:30pm);

buildings close 5pm (Nov–Mar: 4pm)

Adm ¥10 (Nov–Mar ¥5); Yongan Temple and Jade Island cost an extra ¥10 each; combined ticket for park, Yongan Temple and Jade Island ¥20 (Nov–Mar ¥15)

■ There are restaurants on Jade Island and a café beside the White Dagoba.

■ The park has four entry gates: the north gate is the most convenient for the subway, but the south gate makes for a grander entrance.

TOP 10 ⭐ Hou Hai

The area around the joined lakes of Qian Hai and Hou Hai has traditionally been home to nobles and wealthy merchants. Several grand homes survive, hidden in the labyrinthine old lanes known as *hutongs*. This is a rare quarter of Beijing where the 21st century is kept at bay, and these back alleys represent one of the most satisfying parts of the city to explore on foot – or by rickshaw.

① Boating and skating

In summer the lakes are filled with small pedal boats. By mid-December, they are frozen over **(below)** and a large area is cordoned off for ice-skating.

② Silver Ingot Bridge

The narrow channel that connects Hou Hai's two lakes is spanned by the pretty, arched Silver Ingot Bridge, which originally dates from the time of the Yuan dynasty (1279–1368).

③ Former Residence of Guo Moruo

Beijing's many "former residences of" are mostly connected with Party favorites. Moruo was an author and key figure in the rise of Communism in China.

④ Hutongs

The lakes **(above)** lie at the heart of a sprawling old district, characterized by traditional alleyways known as *hutongs*. These alleys are lined for the most part by the blank outer walls of *siheyuan*, which are inward-looking houses arranged around a central courtyard.

⑤ Drum and Bell Towers

Just north of the eastern end of Yandai Xie Jie, these two imposing towers *(see p81)* once rang out the city's nightly curfew. You can ascend the towers for views of the *hutongs*.

8 Rickshaw tours

One way of seeing the *hutongs* is from a rickshaw **(left)**. Prices are negotiable, but expect to pay around ¥180 per person for a two-hour jaunt with the occasional stop-off.

Hou Hai

10 Mansion of Prince Gong

This former residence of Prince Gong is a preserved historic mansion in Beijing. The garden is a pattern of corridors and pavilions, dotted with pools and gates **(below)**.

6 Song Qingling's Residence

Song Qingling was the wife of the revolutionary leader Sun Yat Sen. Her former living quarters are now a small museum. The surrounding gardens are beautiful.

9 Yandai Xie Jie

A bustling lane where tobacco and pipes were once sold, Yandai Xie Jie is lined with historic buildings, most of which have been converted into small bars, snack stalls, and souvenir shops.

7 Lotus Lane

This is Hou Hai's main lakeside parade of restaurants, bars, and cafés **(below)**. Many of these establishments have attractive waterfront terraces.

SIHEYUAN

Traditional Beijing homes, known as *siheyuan*, are arranged around a central courtyard. Originally homes of the well-to-do, over time many *siheyuan* were occupied by poorer families, who squeezed several households into the space formerly occupied by one. Modernization has destroyed many of these dwellings, but there is a movement to preserve those that have survived. A few of them have been converted into chic hotels.

TOP 10 ⭐ Summer Palace (Yiheyuan)

A vast landscaped garden on the edge of the city, this seasonal imperial retreat from the stifling confines of the Forbidden City was the favored haunt of Empress Cixi. She had it rebuilt twice: once after its destruction by French and English troops in 1860, and again in 1902, after it was plundered during the Boxer Rebellion.

1 Hall of Happiness and Longevity

This impressive hall was the residence of the Empress Cixi. It has supposedly been left just as it was at the time of her death in 1908, complete with its Qing dynasty-era furniture.

2 Garden of Virtue and Harmony

This pretty complex of roofed corridors, small pavilions, rock gardens, and pools also includes Cixi's private three-story theater. The buildings now contain Qing-era artifacts, from vehicles to costumes and glassware.

3 Long Corridor

From the Hall of Happiness and Longevity the rather aptly named Long Corridor **(left)** zigzags along the shore of the lake, interrupted along its length by four pavilions. The corridor's ceilings and beams are decorated with over 14,000 scenic paintings.

Summer Palace (Yiheyuan)

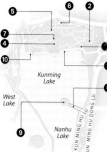

Kunming Lake

West Lake

Nanhu Lake

KUN MING HU LU

KUN MING HU DONG LU

4 Tower of Buddhist Incense

Toward the peak of Longevity Hill rises this octagonal tower. The stiff climb is rewarded with views over the roofs of the halls and pavilions to the lake below.

7 Temple of the Sea of Wisdom

North of the Tower of Buddhist Incense is a tiled temple decorated with 1,008 miniature Buddha statues set in niches on the outer walls **(left)**.

5 Longevity Hill

At around the half-way point of the Long Corridor, a series of buildings ascends the slopes of Longevity Hill **(below)**. The start of the sequence is marked at the lakeside by a fine decorative gate.

6 Suzhou Street

This shopping street was built for the amusement of the Qianlong emperor, his concubines and eunuchs, who would play at being shoppers, shopkeepers, and pickpockets.

EMPRESS CIXI

Cixi is remembered as one of China's most powerful women. Having borne one emperor's son as an imperial concubine, she became the power behind the throne to two more: her son and her nephew. When she blocked state reforms and lent support to the xenophobic Boxers in their rebellion *(see p38)*, she unwittingly paved the way for the end of the imperial era.

8 Seventeen-Arch Bridge

South Lake Island is linked to the eastern shore by a bridge **(below)** with a lion crowning each of the 544 balusters along its length, all supposedly individual. The bronze ox was installed on the shore to quell floods.

9 South Lake Island

Crowning this island on Kunming Lake is the Dragon King Temple (Longwang Miao), which is dedicated to the god of rivers, seas, and rain.

10 Marble Boat

The wooden structure of the boat is painted white to look like marble. Boat trips to South Lake Island depart from a neighboring jetty.

NEED TO KNOW

6 miles (10 km) NW of central Beijing ▪ 6288 1144 ▪ Subway: Beigongmen, Xiyuan, Yiheyuan Ximen ▪ www. summer palace-china.com

Open Apr–Oct: 6:30am–8pm (park) daily, 8:30am–5pm (sights) daily; Nov–Mar: 7am–7pm (park) daily, 9am–4pm (sights) daily; the last admission is two hours before closing

Adm ¥60 all inclusive (Nov–Mar ¥50); ¥30 park only (Nov–Mar ¥20); audio guides are available for ¥40 (plus ¥50 deposit)

▪ There are several small snack kiosks situated in the park grounds.

▪ Avoid visiting on days with poor visibility when you risk missing the superb views across the Summer Palace lake.

798 Art District

Since the first artists set up in Da Shan Zi's newly vacated 798 factory in 2001, the 1950s East German-built industrial compound has become a world-famous center of contemporary Chinese art. Alongside the studios and galleries, there are also chic cafés, bars, and restaurants, not to mention a growing number of designer shops and showrooms. Popular with hipsters, the area has seen increasing gentrification.

Maoist graffiti

When many of the abandoned factory spaces in the district were being converted and refurbished for use as art galleries, the artists instructed the decorators to leave untouched the giant Maoist slogans that had been lettered on the walls by the former workers at the 798 factory.

Vibrant graffiti art in the 798 Art District

2 M Woods Art Museum

Run by prominent Chinese art collectors, this labyrinth of inter-connected warehouse spaces stages multi-artist shows curated on changing themes, including Austin Lee's Human Nature **(above)**.

3 Long March Space

Supporting emerging artists since 2002, curator Lu Jie's gallery is one of the best in the 798 Art District for Chinese contemporary painting, sculpture, and video installations.

4 AT Café

This fashionable café's notable feature is a bare-brick wall punctured by massive holes **(right)**. It is owned by artist Huang Rui, who was instrumental in preventing the factory-turned-art-zone from being demolished in 2004.

5 Galleria Continua

Beijing's outpost of this Italian gallery, in a former munitions factory, aims to stimulate cultural exchanges. It hosts shows by renowned international artists such as Chen Zhen, Antony Gormley, Daniel Buren, and Anish Kapoor.

798 Art District

BRAVE NEW WORLDS

1985 marked the arrival of the avant garde in Chinese art, with controversial student graduation shows igniting intense debate in artistic circles. A year later, a New York gallery introduced the new Chinese art to an international audience. Today, China's art market is the second largest in the world after the US.

7 UCCA

The Ullens Center for Contemporary Art (UCCA) **(below)** is the largest single venue in this area, and exhibits an eclectic range of big-name international artists. UCCA has an auditorium for lectures and films, a store, and a restaurant.

9 Faurschou Foundation

A relative newcomer, this privately owned Danish gallery has hosted exhibitions by the likes of French-American artist Louise Bourgeois, Chinese artist Cai Guo-Qiang, and Japanese artist Yoko Ono.

6 Timezone 8

This is a trendy Western and Japanese restaurant that serves imported beers, saké and *sochu*. A popular hangout, it has a pleasant terrace, ideal for people-watching.

8 Beijing Commune

This Bauhaus-style brick building has been promoting aspiring Chinese artists since 2004. It primarily focuses on solo performances.

10 Magician Space

This small avant-garde gallery with a pioneering spirit has hosted a solo exhibition by the controversial Chinese artist Ai Weiwei.

NEED TO KNOW

2–4 Jiu Xian Qiao Lu, Da Shan Zi, Chaoyang ■ Subway: Wanjing South, Jiangtai, then walk north for 15 min ■ Bus: 401, 402, 405, 418, 445, 955, 973, 988, 991

To Caochangdi: Bus 418 from Dong Zhi Men

Galleria Continua: 5978 9505; open 11am–6pm Tue–Sun; www.galleria continua.com

UCCA: 5780 0200; open 10am–7pm Tue–Sun; adm ¥60–100; www. ucca.org.cn

Beijing Commune: 8456 2862; open 10am–6pm Tue–Sat; www. beijingcommune.com

Faurschou Foundation: 5978 9316; open 10am–6pm Tue–Sat; www.faurschou.com

Magician Space: 5978 9635; open 10:30am–6:30pm Tue–Sun; magician-space.com

■ Most galleries are open from around 11am to 7pm, and are closed on Mondays.

🔟 ⭐ Ming Tombs

The resting place for 13 of the 16 Ming-dynasty (1368–1644) emperors, this is China's finest example of imperial funerary architecture. The site was chosen because of its auspicious feng shui alignment: a ridge of mountains to the north cradles the tombs on three sides, protecting the dead from the evil spirits carried on the north wind. The tombs are spread over 15 square miles (40 sq km). Three (Chang Ling, Ding Ling, and Zhao Ling) have been restored and accept visitors. The others are not open to the public.

1 Stele Pavilion
At the tunnel-like arch of the Stele Pavilion, the largest stele in China projects from the shell of a giant bixi (dragon-tortoise) and bears the names of the emperors buried at the site.

3 Spirit Tower
Rising up from the third courtyard of the Chang Ling complex, this tower marks the entrance to the burial chamber. It takes the form of an earthen tumulus girdled by a wall.

2 Memorial Arch
Marking the entrance to the site is a five-arched marble gate **(above)** built in 1540. At 40 ft (12 m) high and more than 92 ft (28 m) wide, it is the largest of its kind in China, and has beautiful carvings.

4 Ding Ling Treasures
A collection of precious artifacts and relics from the Wanli emperor's tomb (the Ding Ling) have been placed in the Hall of Eminent Favor.

NEED TO KNOW

30 miles (45 km) NW of Beijing ▪ 6076 1424 ▪ Subway to Ming Tombs station, then bus 949 to Dagongmen stop or 872 from Beijing Deshengmen ▪ www.mingtombs.com

Open Apr–Oct: 8am–5:30pm daily; Nov–Mar: 8:30am–5pm daily

Adm Chang Ling ¥45 (¥30 off-peak), Ding Ling ¥60 (¥40 off-peak), Zhao Ling ¥30 (¥20 off-peak); Combo ticket ¥130 (¥100 off-peak)

▪ The Ming Tombs can also be covered as part of a trip to the Great Wall at Badaling. Many hotels are able to arrange tours to the site.

▪ Bus 872 leaves Desheng Men Bus Terminal every 10 minutes (9:15am–4:15pm) to Changling and Dingling (¥10). The last return bus is at 6pm.

▪ It's advisable to bring your own packed lunch.

Ming Tombs

5 Chang Ling Tomb

The resting place **(below)** of the Yongle emperor, builder of the Forbidden City and Temple of Heaven, is the oldest and grandest tomb. It is well restored, but the chamber where Yongle, his wife, and 16 concubines are buried has never been excavated.

7 Zhao Ling Tomb

This is the final resting place of the Longqing emperor (1537–72). The 13th emperor of the Ming dynasty, he gained the throne at the age of 30 and died six years later. The tomb has an attractive triple-bridge built over a stream. It is closed for renovation.

9 Spirit Way

Part of the 4-mile (7-km) approach to the tombs, the Spirit Way is lined with 18 pairs of giant guardians **(above)** – stone statues of imperial warriors, court officials, animals, and Chinese mythical beasts.

10 Ding Ling Burial Chamber

This is the only burial chamber to be excavated and opened to the public. It holds three red-lacquer coffins, belonging to Wanli and his two wives.

6 Ding Ling Tomb

This is the tomb of the longest-reigning Ming emperor, Wanli (1573–1620). His profligate rule initiated the downfall of the dynasty. His tomb **(below)** took six years to build, and its impressive structure is representative of the emperor's extravagant lifestyle.

8 Hall of Eminent Favor

One of China's most impressive surviving Ming buildings, this double-eaved sacrificial hall is the centerpiece of the Chang Ling tomb complex. It stands on a triple-tiered marble terrace and 32 gigantic cedar columns support its hipped roof.

THE MING DYNASTY

The 276-year Ming ("brilliant") dynasty rule was one of the longest and most stable periods in Chinese history. The founder of the Ming dynasty rose from humble beginnings via military successes to become emperor. He was succeeded by his grandson, who in turn was succeeded by his son, who proclaimed himself emperor Yongle ("Eternal Joy"). It was Yongle who moved the capital from Nanjing to Beijing, where he created a new city.

🔟 ⭐ Great Wall of China

The Great Wall of China snakes over deserts, hills, and plains for several thousand miles. At its closest point it is less than 40 miles (65 km) from Beijing. Building first began after the unification of China under Qin Shi Huangdi (221–210 BC), and more construction continued for over 2,000 years. The impressive brick battlements seen in the mountains north of Beijing are around 500 years old, erected during the Ming dynasty.

Great Wall of China snaking through lush hills

1 Badaling
The Ming fortification at Badaling was the first section to be restored for tourists. Its accessibility means it is perpetually busy, but it is possible to escape the crowds by walking along the wall. Badaling can be reached from Beijing by bullet train in 20 minutes.

2 Great Wall Museum
Housed in an imitation Qing dynasty building at Badaling, this museum **(left)** presents the entire history of the region as well as details about the construction and military aspects of the wall.

3 Simatai
East of Jinshanling, the steep battlements at Simatai were restored in 2014. A stretch of this section of the wall is lit up at sundown and can be safely climbed after sunset.

NEED TO KNOW

Badaling: 44 miles (70 km) NW of Beijing; 6912 1383; train from Beijing North Station; bus 877 from Deshengmen; open 6:30am–7pm daily (Nov–Mar: 7am–6pm daily); adm ¥45; www.ticket.badaling.cn

Xizhazi (Jiankou): 60 miles (96 km) N of Beijing;

private car and driver around ¥1,200 per day

Mutianyu: 56 miles (90 km) N of Beijing; 6162 6505; bus 916 from Dong Zhi Men station, change to taxi at Huairou; open 7:30am–6pm Mon–Fri, 7:30am–6:30pm Sat & Sun (Nov–Mar: 8am–5pm daily); adm ¥40

Huanghua Cheng: 37 miles (60 km) N of Beijing;

6165 1044; bus 916 to Huairou station, then bus H2114 to Small West Lake station; open 8:30am–5pm Mon–Fri, 8:30am–4:30pm daily); adm ¥45

Juyong Guan: open 8am–5pm daily (Nov–Mar: 8:30am–4pm daily); adm ¥45 (Nov–Mar: ¥40)

4 Juyong Guan

This is the closest accessible part of the wall to Beijing. With unscalable mountains on either side it is easy to see why the spot was chosen for defence. Early cannons remain on the ramparts. Also worth seeing are Buddhist carvings on a stone platform, or "cloud terrace," in the middle of the pass.

7 Xizhazi

This village in the less-developed Jiankou area affords spectacular views and wild hikes to unrestored parts of the Great Wall. Xizhazi's local guesthouses offer fresh, country-style dining and a night on a traditional *kang* (heated bed).

> **VISITING THE WALL**
>
> Most hotels are able to organize a trip to the wall, sometimes combined with a visit to the Ming Tombs (see pp32–3). Try to find out whether there are any unwanted diversions to jade factories, cloisonné workshops, or Chinese medicine clinics. Small groups can see more remote parts of the wall, by hiring a car and driver for the day from Beijing. Hiking clubs in Beijing offer day trips to lesser-known parts of the wall.

5 Gubeikou

This pass offers some of the best hiking trails to the unrestored parts of the Great Wall. Trek 7 miles (12 km), with a guide or a group, along the wall to Jinshanling.

8 Shanhaiguan

The wall ends (or begins) at the sea **(above)**. East of town, the "First Pass Under Heaven" is a formidable section of wall attached to a gatehouse. A good destination if you want to do an overnight trip.

9 Mutianyu

In a dramatic hilly setting, and with a series of watchtowers along its restored length, the wall here dates from 1368. Local village buildings have now been converted into both holiday homes and restaurants.

6 Jinshanling

Barren, lofty, and remote, the restored battlements at Jinshanling **(below)** are particularly dense in watchtowers, and reveal many bricks inscribed with the makers' marks and date stamps.

10 Huanghua Cheng

Known as the "Lakeside Great Wall", this stunning tourist zone offers spectacular views, pleasure boating, ornamental gardens, and the chance to see some sections of the Great Wall partially submerged in the waters of a reservoir. Unrestored sections nearby are popular with hikers, however, access is often restricted.

The Top 10 of Everything

**Performers on stage during
a Beijing Opera show**

🔟 Moments in History

① 500,000 BC: Peking Man Hunts and Gathers

Unearthed in the 1920s from a cave at Zhoukoudian, 30 miles (45 km) southwest of Beijing, 40-odd fossilized bones and primitive implements were identified as the remains of Peking Man *(Homo erectus Pekinensis)*, who lived in the vicinity over 500,000 years ago.

② 1215: Genghis Khan Sacks Zhongdu

The future Beijing was developed as an auxiliary capital under the Liao (907–1125) and Jin (1115–1234) dynasties, at which time it was known as Zhongdu. In 1215 it was invaded and razed by a Mongol army led by the fearsome Genghis Khan.

③ Late 13th Century: Marco Polo Visits

Under the Mongol Yuan dynasty's first emperor, Kublai Khan (r. 1260–94), the city became known as Khanbalik, and was one of twin capitals – the other was Yuanshangdu, or Xanadu – of the largest empire ever known.

Kublai Khan, of the Mongol Yuan dynasty

The Venetian traveler Marco Polo was dazzled by the imperial palace: "No man on earth could design anything superior to it."

④ 1403–20: Construction of the Forbidden City

The Ming emperor Yongle (r. 1403–24) destroyed the palaces of his Mongol predecessors in order to rebuild the city, which he renamed Beijing (Northern Capital). He is credited with laying the foundations for the city as it is today, and the Forbidden City and Temple of Heaven began to take shape during his reign.

⑤ 1900: Boxer Rebellion

Western powers, frustrated by the reluctance of the Chinese to open up to foreign trade, put the imperial court under pressure, eventually going to war to protect their trade in opium. In 1900, championed by the Empress Cixi, a band of rebels known as the Boxers attacked Beijing's Foreign Legation Quarter. A joint eight-nation army had to be sent to lift the siege.

Violent clashes during the Boxer Rebellion of 1900

6 1912: The End of Empire

The last emperor, Pu Yi, was only three years old when he ascended the throne. Four years later, in February 1912, he was forced to abdicate by general Yuan Shikai's new National Assembly.

7 1949: Founding of the People's Republic of China

In January 1949, Communist forces led by Mao Zedong seized Beijing. On October 1, Mao proclaimed the People's Republic of China from the gallery of the Tian'an Men.

Mao's 1965 Cultural Revolution

8 1965: Launch of the Cultural Revolution

Having socialized industry and agriculture, Mao called on the masses to transform society itself. All distinctions between manual and intellectual work were to be abolished and the class system was to be eradicated. The revolution reached its violent peak in 1967, with the Red Guards spreading fear and havoc.

9 1976: The Death of Mao

On September 9, 1976 Mao died. His long-time opponent Deng Xiaoping became leader, implementing reforms that encouraged greater economic freedom.

10 2022: Beijing Hosts Second Olympics

Fourteen years after Beijing's successful hosting of the 2008 Summer Olympic Games, the iconic Bird's Nest and Water Cube were put to action once again to host the 2022 Winter Olympics.

TOP 10 CHINESE INVENTIONS

Chinese magnetic compass

1 Magnetic compass
Developed from an instrument used for feng shui and geomancy, it helped the Chinese explore the world.

2 Printing
In the 11th century, the Chinese carved individual characters on pieces of clay, inventing movable block type.

3 Paper money
This was developed by Chinese merchants as certificates of exchange. Lighter than coins, bills were soon adopted by the government.

4 Gunpowder
Stumbled on by Daoist alchemists seeking the elixir of life.

5 Seismometer
A ball fell from one of four dragons' mouths to indicate the direction of the earthquake.

6 Abacus
Invented during the Yuan dynasty and still in use in parts of China today.

7 Porcelain
The Chinese invented porcelain 1,000 years before Europe caught on – and kept production methods secret to protect their competitive advantage.

8 Paper
A prototype paper was made from mulberry bark, although bamboo, hemp, linen, and silk were also used to write on.

9 Crossbow
Better range, accuracy, and penetration than the standard bow.

10 Decimal system
Developed alongside the writing system, the decimal system led to mathematical advances.

🔟 Places of Worship

Pavilion in the Confucius Temple

1 Confucius Temple (Kong Miao)

An enormous complex of wooden halls and flagstoned courtyards, the Confucius Temple *(see p82)* is popular with visitors and pays testament to the revival of Confucian ethics in modern China. A museum inside the temple holds artifacts of the Imperial civil service exams, and Confucian texts.

2 South Cathedral

Officially known as the Cathedral of the Immaculate Conception, this *(see p76)* was the first Catholic house of worship in Beijing. It is the largest functioning church, and has regular services in a variety of languages including Mandarin, English, and Latin. Service times are posted on the noticeboard.

3 St. Joseph's Church

MAP N3 ▪ 74 Wangfujing Dajie ▪ 6524 0634 ▪ Subway: Dengshikou

Also known as the East Cathedral, this is a triple-domed church in the Baroque style. It was first built on the site of the residence of a Jesuit missionary in 1655 and, following earthquakes, fire, and the Boxer Rebellion *(see p38)*, has been rebuilt multiple times. It is fronted by a gateway and piazza, and surrounded by the shopping malls of Wangfujing. Mass is held in English on Sundays at 4pm.

4 Wanshou Temple

MAP A1 ▪ Xisanhuan Lu, on the north side of Zizhu Qiao Bridge ▪ 6842 3565 ▪ Subway: Xizhi Men, then bus 300, 360, or 361 ▪ Open 9am–4pm Tue–Sun ▪ Adm

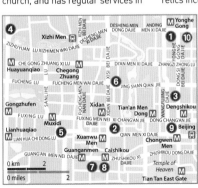

Incense burner at Wanshou Temple

In the northwest Haidian District, the Wanshou (Longevity) Temple is worth a stop en route to the Summer Palace. The complex houses the Beijing Art Museum – a collection of historical relics including bronzes, jade, carved lacquer, and a small but exquisite collection of Buddha images.

5 White Cloud Temple

Founded in AD 739, this is Beijing's largest Daoist shrine *(see p95)*. Daoism, also known as Taoism, is a Chinese folk religion, which centers around maintaining a positive relationship with several categories of gods, ghosts, and ancestral spirits.

Facade of the Gothic North Cathedral

10th century, it's an unusual hybrid of Chinese and Islamic architecture, with its entrance facing west rather than the customary south.

8 Fayuan Temple

This temple *(see p74)* doubles as a Buddhist Academy. Founded in 1956, the Academy trains monks to serve in monasteries throughout China. The temple has an excellent collection of sculptures, including a giant reclining Buddha.

9 St. Michael's Church

MAP N5 ▪ 13 Dong Jiao Min Xiang ▪ 6513 5170 ▪ Subway: Chongwen Men

This is one of the city's lesser-known churches, hidden away in the old Legation Quarter *(see p76)*. It was built in 1901 to serve the area's various embassies. Narrowly escaping destruction during the Cultural Revolution, it was renovated by the Chinese Patriotic Catholic Church.

6 North Cathedral

MAP J2 ▪ 33 Xishiku Dajie ▪ Subway: Xisi

The white-trimmed grey facade of this cathedral, a twin-towered piece of Gothic confectionery, masks a bloody past: not long after the Jesuits finished the church in 1889, it came under siege during the Boxer Rebellion *(see p38)*. Many of the congregation sheltering inside were killed.

7 Niu Jie Mosque

The largest population of Beijing's Chinese Muslims live in the Niu Jie District, which is a busy area with halal butchers, bakers, and restaurants. The mosque *(see p76)* is the city's oldest and largest Islamic place of worship. Founded around the

10 Lama Temple

One of the most notable centers of Tibetan Buddhism outside Tibet until it was shut down during the Cultural Revolution, this temple *(see pp20–21)* was saved from destruction by the intervention of the then president, Zhou Enlai. The precincts are home to a small number of monks.

Gilded statues at the Lama Temple, an important Buddhist center

🔟 Museums

3 Overseas Chinese History Museum

MAP F1 ■ Beixinqiao Santiao Dongkou ■ Subway: Beixinqiao ■ Open 9am–5pm Tue–Sun ■ Passport required

This impressive museum uses lifelike dioramas to present the history of Chinese emigration from the Silk Road era right up to the present.

1 National Museum of China

Dedicated to Chinese history and arts, this gargantuan museum beside Tian'an Men Square (see p70) documents the evolution of Chinese civilization through the country's most important historic and cultural artifacts. The museum showcases China's rise in the face of adversity.

4 Poly Art Museum

MAP G2 ■ Floor 9, New Poly Plaza, 1 Chaoyang Men Bei Dajie, Dongcheng District ■ 6500 1188 ■ Open 9:30am–4:30pm Mon–Sat ■ Adm

Hidden inside an office block, this museum linked to an auction house has a stellar collection of ancient bronzes and Buddhist statuary, artfully displayed on lit plinths.

5 Imperial City Art Museum

Call by this museum near the Forbidden City (see p70) to see all the bits of imperial Beijing that didn't survive. The walls and gates that once encircled the city, along with dozens of vanished temples, are revisited through a great many maps, models, and photographs.

Natural History Museum

2 Natural History Museum

The museum (see p77) has around 5,000 fascinating specimens on display, including a collection of models and skeletons of dinosaurs, and other prehistoric creatures.

6 Beijing Police Museum

MAP M6 ■ 36 Dong Jiao Min Xiang ■ 8522 5018 ■ Subway: Qian Men ■ Open 9am–4pm Tue–Sun

Housed in the 1914 former City Bank of New York, this surprisingly fun museum tells the story of Beijing's PSB (Public Security Bureau) with displays on themes such as the suppression of drug dealers and counter-revolutionaries. Famed police dog Feisheng is stuffed and mounted and there are also gruesome displays of Qing dynasty law enforcement and punishment methods.

The modern building housing the Capital Museum

7 Capital Museum

In a large, modern five-story building near Fuxingmen, this museum (see p94) documents Beijing's history through over 200,000 relics and archival images. The highlight is the timeline exhibit charting Beijing's evolution from the Jin Dynasty to the present.

8 National Art Museum of China

The largest art museum in the country, with an impressive 64,580 sq ft (6,000 sq m) of floor space, the National Art Museum of China (see p70) hosts exhibitions which feature a vast number of works of both Chinese and international artists. There are usually four exhibitions *in situ* at any one time, with full listings published on the museum's website. Passport required for entry.

9 Ancient Architecture Museum

Close to the Temple of Heaven, south of Tian'an Men Square, this place (see p77) is worth a visit for the museum building alone, which is the pavilion of a former grand temple complex.

Exhibit at the Military Museum

10 Military Museum of the Chinese People's Revolution

Visitors to this museum (see p96) are greeted by paintings of Mao, Marx, Lenin, and Stalin, at least two of whom were responsible for inflicting the horrific levels of death and destruction depicted within the museum. The main gallery is packed to the rafters with planes, tanks, and bombs, while side galleries chronicle China's military campaigns.

National Art Museum of China

TOP10 The Olympic Legacy

The iconic architecture of the National Olympic Stadium (Bird's Nest)

1 Ice Ribbon

More formally known as the National Speed Skating Oval, this futuristic arena was the only new venue built at the Olympic Green for Beijing's hosting of the 2022 Winter Olympics.

National Aquatics Center/Water Cube

2 National Aquatics Center/Water Cube

Inspired by bubbles and molecules, the dramatic-looking Water Cube (see p49) hosted the swimming and diving events of the 2008 games. For the 2022 Winter Olympics, it hosted the curling and was rechristened the Ice Cube.

3 National Indoor Stadium

Built to host gymnastics and handball during the 2008 Games, this stadium has a curving roof with slatted beams, inspired by Chinese folding fans. Post-Olympics, it stages entertainment events.

4 National Olympic Stadium (Bird's Nest)

Designed in collaboration with the Chinese artist Ai Weiwei, the National Olympic Stadium is an architectural icon. Its outer ribbons of structural steel resemble the woven twigs of a bird's nest as they loop and swirl over the 91,000-seat arena, hence the building's nickname.

5 Olympic Green

The vast Olympic Green surrounds the Olympic Village and extends beyond the fifth ring road. At its heart is a dragon-shaped lake, as well as waterfalls, meadows, and streams. Entry is free.

6 Olympic Green Convention Center

This building hosted the fencing events during the Games, as well as providing a home for the International Broadcasting Center. Its distinctive shape mirrors the traditional Chinese "flying roof" and acts as a giant rainwater collector. The building is now a multipurpose conference center.

7 Beijing Airport, Terminal 3

One of the world's largest and most advanced airport buildings, Lord Norman Foster's Terminal 3 welcomed international athletes to the 2008 Olympics. The design resembles a soaring dragon in red and yellow, thus evoking traditional Chinese colors and symbols.

8 National Center for the Performing Arts
MAP K5

French architect Paul Andreu's silvery "Egg" *(see p70)* provides a striking contrast to the monolithic Socialist architecture of neighboring Tian'an Men Square. The building is surrounded by a reflective moat and accessed by an underwater tunnel.

9 Wukesong Arena

Rebranded since the Olympics, the host venue for the basketball games features a unique exterior design that gives the impression of movement, with boards alternately rising and falling. More than mere show, the aluminum alloy boards reflect heat and reportedly result in 60–70 per cent energy savings. The arena hosted a number of ice-hockey matches for the 2022 Winter Olympics.

10 CCTV Building
MAP H4

The most striking addition to the Beijing skyline after the 2008 games was the headquarters of China Central Television. Designed by Dutch architects Rem Koolhaas and Ole Scheeren, it is a gravity-defying loop that pushes the limits of architecture. Its unusual design has prompted some locals to nickname the building "Big Pants" (trousers).

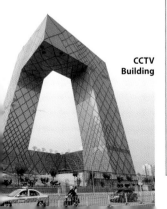

CCTV Building

TOP 10 CHINESE SOCIALIST ARCHITECTURE

Great Hall of the People

1 Great Hall of the People
MAP L5
This 1959 Soviet-style building features on the ¥100 note.

2 Agricultural Exhibition Center
MAP H2
In 1959, for the tenth anniversary of the People's Republic of China, this was one of ten buildings commissioned.

3 National Museum of China
This museum *(see p70)* is housed in an imposing 1950s Soviet-style building.

4 Beijing Railway Station
MAP F4
Prime illustration of 1959's "size is everything" approach to architecture.

5 Cultural Palace of the Nationalities
MAP C4
The one "tenth-anniversary" building of elegance. Its plan forms the Chinese character for "mountain."

6 Minzu Hotel
MAP C4
No Chinese motifs here – but it's suitably monolithic and drab.

7 Military Museum of the Chinese People's Revolution
MAP A4
Owes a striking debt to Moscow.

8 Natural History Museum
MAP E6
Neo-Classical Socialist Chinese – but fairly nice once you're inside.

9 National Art Museum of China
MAP M2
Mao himself penned the calligraphy on this museum's facade.

10 Beijing West Railway Station
MAP A5
A 1995 take on 1959-style architecture.

🔟 Off The Beaten Path

1 White Cloud Temple

Built in AD 739, this Taoist temple *(see p95)* houses the China Taoist Association and 30 monks with their distinctive robes and top knots. It usually sees more pilgrims than tourists and has elaborate halls and gates, as well as three stone monkeys – finding them all is said to bring good luck.

3 Ancient Observatory

Located in a watchtower, this is one of the world's oldest observatories *(see p89)*. Among the many artifacts on display here are replicas of the old navigational tools that enabled Ming dynasty travelers to explore the world.

Sundial, Ancient Observatory

4 Beijing Shijingshan Amusement Park

Shijingshan Road, Shijingshan District ■ 8892 5159 ■ Subway: Bajiao Youleyuan ■ Open 9am–4:30pm daily (to 5pm Sat & Sun) ■ Adm; free for children under 6 years or 4 ft (1.2 m)

Beijing's oldest amusement park may not have the high-tech rides, but it is considerably cheaper, and less crowded. The rides here are fun nonetheless, and it has a certain kitsch charm. The park is divided into themed districts offering several entertainment facilities, including parades, shows and performances.

Inside the Watermelon Museum

2 The Watermelon Museum

Pangge Zhuang Town, Daxing District ■ 8928 1181 ■ Subway: Tiangongyuan ■ Open 8am–5:30pm Mon–Fri ■ Adm

Located to the far south of Beijing, the Watermelon Museum is a surrealist modern Socialist museum. China is the world's biggest exporter of watermelons, and self-pick farms surround this gleaming temple to the famous fruit. Although there aren't any signs in English anywhere, you can get the gist of the exhibits.

5 Beijing Botanical Gardens

If the hustle and bustle of the city gets to be too much, surround yourself with Chinese roses, peach blossoms, and peonies. The massive greenhouse here *(see p100)* displays more than 3,000 varieties of flora, ranging from tropical to desert. Pu Yi, the last emperor, worked here briefly in the 1960s as a gardener.

Beijing Botanical Gardens in full bloom

Bronze lion at Fayuan Temple

⑨ Poly Art Museum

The silent, richly carpeted rooms at the Poly Art Museum *(see p40)* hold a wealth of stone, ceramic, and bronze statuary. Highlights include four bronze animals rescued from the 19th-century sacking of the Summer Palace, as well as artifacts ranging from the Shang to the Tang dynasties and earlier.

⑩ Beijing Eunuch Museum (Tian Yi Mu)

80 Moshi Kou Dajie, Shijing Shan District ▪ 8872 4148 ▪ Subway: Jin'anqiao ▪ Open 8:30am–4:30pm daily ▪ Adm

In the 16th century, the eunuch Tian Yi, who carried his genitals in a jug, served three emperors of the Ming dynasty. Over time, he achieved an elevated position at court, and when he died, in 1605, his funeral generated three days of silence in the Forbidden City. Tian Yi's elaborately carved tomb is now empty, having been raided during China's Cultural Revolution. However, this interesting museum houses a range of murals, monuments, marble phalluses, and a diorama of the castration process, which was performed without anesthetic drugs.

⑥ Fayuan Temple

A visit to Fayuan Temple *(see p74)* offers the opportunity to observe the fascinating daily life of a monk. Built in AD 696 by Tang dynasty emperor Tai Zong to mourn fallen soldiers, Fayuan is likely Beijing's oldest Buddhist temple.

⑦ Qianding Old Liquor Museum

MAP E2 ▪ 44 Yandai Xiejie, Dongcheng District ▪ Subway: Gulou Dajie ▪ Open 9am–6pm Tue–Sun ▪ Adm

This museum is all about *baijiu* (traditional grain alcohol) through the ages, and on display are more than 1,600 varieties of the stuff. It's on a busy lane between the Drum Tower and Hou Hai.

⑧ The Former Residence of Guo Moruo

Guo Moruo was a 20th-century writer, poet, dramatist, historian, archeologist, and paleographer, as well as an enthusiastic gardener. Much of his outdoor handiwork survives here *(see p26)*, his former home, in addition to piles of manuscripts, books, and a bronze statue of the man himself.

TOP 10 Children's Attractions

Display at the Natural History Museum

① Natural History Museum

There's plenty to keep curious over 5-year-olds entertained here, including animatronic dinosaurs, prehistoric skeletons, and stuffed animals of all sizes *(see p77)*.

② Latitude

Anping Street, Houshayu, near Beijing Capital International Airport ▪ 8047 6556 ▪ Subway: Houshayu ▪ Open 10am–9pm Mon–Fri, 9am–10pm Sat & Sun ▪ Adm

Ideal for older kids, this indoor gym features trampolining, rock climbing, beam battle and dodge ball amongst a host of other thrilling activities. A great way to get the whole family active.

③ Beijing Aquarium

MAP B2 ▪ 108 Gao Liang Qiao Xijie ▪ 6217 6655 ▪ Open 9am–5:30pm daily (Nov–Mar: 10am–4:30pm daily) ▪ Adm ▪ www.bj-sea.com

Located in the northeastern corner of Beijing Zoo, this vast aquarium will keep children happy for hours.

④ New China Children's Store

MAP N4 ▪ 168 Wangfujing Dajie ▪ 6528 1774 ▪ Subway: Wangfujing ▪ Open 9am–9:30pm daily

A four-storied children's store on Beijing's main shopping street, with everything from carry-cots and strollers to local and imported toys. There's even an in-store play area.

⑤ Happy Valley

Xiaowuji Bei Lu, East 4th Ring Road ▪ 6738 3333 ▪ Subway: Huanlegu Jingqu ▪ Open 9:30am–10pm daily ▪ Adm; children under 3.6 ft (1.1 m) free

This Disneyland-style park has 120 attractions over six themed regions. Thrill-seekers can enjoy no fewer than 40 rides, of which ten are "extreme," including a "Drop Tower" in which riders fall at 45 mph (72 km/h) in a terrifying simulated plunge to earth. There is also a shopping complex, and an IMAX cinema.

Thrilling ride at Happy Valley

Carousel at Hamleys

6 Hamleys
255 Wangfujing Dajie
■ 6526 6108 ■ Subway: Wangfujing
■ Open 10am–10pm daily
This five-story outpost of London's famous toy store is a hands-on delight for little ones. A ride-on train trundles through the aisles and there's even a merry-go-round on the ground floor.

7 Mutianyu Great Wall
One of the best-preserved sections of the Great Wall of China, Mutianyu (see p34) provides spectacular views and an easy climb for families with older kids. A cable-car and chairlift will rescue tired legs, and there's even a short but thrilling toboggan ride that zooms down the hillside.

8 Chaoyang Park
Subway: Liangmaqiao
There are plenty of rides and activities at this exciting park, including roller-coasters and bathing pools, for both children and adults. This is one of the few parks in the city where visitors walk, run, do yoga, kick balls, or lay down on real grass by the lake. Go early, take a picnic, and enjoy the day.

9 Kerry Center Adventure Zone
MAP H4 ■ Kerry Center Hotel, 1 Guanghua Lu ■ 8565 2490 ■ Subway: Guomao ■ Open 10am–9pm Mon–Fri, 9am–10pm Sat & Sun ■ Adm
Parents and children can play together at this fun center with a three-story jungle gym, a tree house, vertical slides, and colorful cars. All areas are age specific, and weary adults can always take a break to relax at the nearby café.

Science and Technology Museum

10 Science and Technology Museum
This museum (see p101) has lots of hands-on exhibits for kids to pull, push, and even walk through. There is also an IMAX-style movie theater and an indoor play area in a separate building north of the main entrance.

TOP 10 Entertainment

A demonstration of martial arts by Shaolin monks

1 Martial Arts

The Shaolin monks from Songshan in Henan Province have gained an international reputation for their martial arts prowess. Periodically, traveling troupes of monks perform in theaters around Beijing.

2 Acrobatics

China is renowned for the quality of its gymnasts, who perform breathtaking routines that showcase their unnerving flexibility. Displays of balance often involve props such as chairs, plates, and bicycles. Several Beijing theaters put on shows – for instance, the Chaoyang Theater; your hotel can help with reservations.

Acrobats on a bicycle

3 Cinema

Most Beijing shopping malls have a modern cineplex inside, typically showing at least one Hollywood blockbuster in English alongside a line-up of Chinese movies. In lieu of a certificate system, Chinese censors scenes deemed not suitable for a general audience.

4 Puppet Theater

Shadow-puppet theater is an art form that has been performed more or less unchanged in China since the 3rd century AD. Shows employ many of the story lines and musical styles of Beijing Opera, while the puppets can be quite elaborate and colorfully dressed. The best place to catch a performance is at the China Puppet Art Theater (*Anhua Xili, off Bei Sanhuan Lu*) in Chaoyang District.

5 Rock and Pop

Beijing has a thriving music scene supported by a host of small music bars and clubs (*see p59*). Punk and metal thrive, and for those with a more eclectic taste, local folk rockers mix traditional Chinese instrumentation with Western genres.

6 Sports

Soccer is big in Beijing. The local boys are Beijing Guo'an, who play in the Chinese Super League at the Workers' Stadium (*see p90*). Book tickets ahead or you might have to buy from a tout outside. Second in popularity is basketball. Aoshen, the top team, plays at the Beijing Guang'an Gymnasium *(Baiguang Lu; Map C6)*.

7 Traditional Music

If you can, attend a traditional Chinese orchestral performance. Sections of unfamiliar plucked string, bowed string, woodwind, and percussion instruments compete for attention in swirling arrangements. The main venues are the Forbidden City Concert Hall in Zhong Shan Park and the National Center for the Performing Arts *(see p70)*.

Performance of traditional music

8 Beijing Opera

With its incomprehensible plots, unfamiliar sounds, and performances lasting up to three hours, Beijing Opera is an acquired taste. Everyone should try it at least once *(see pp52–3)*.

9 Chinese Folk Dances

Performances showcasing China's 56 ethnic minorities, or nationalities, feature traditional costumes and dances. Some shows are truly outstanding, such as Yang Liping's famous peacock dance.

10 Theater

Beijing is home to several excellent theaters, where a few established troupes perform regularly. Canonical works such as Lao She's "Teahouse" are increasingly supplemented by big-budget Western musicals such as "Rent" and "Aladdin on Ice." See the English-language press for what's on.

TOP 10 PARKS

1 Bei Hai Park
Classic ornamental gardens *(see pp24–5)* with a large lake for boating.

2 Chaoyang Park
The largest afforested park *(see p49)* in Beijing.

3 Di Tan Park
Large green spaces and cypress trees, and the striking Altar of Earth *(see p83)*.

4 Xiang Shan Park
Twelve miles (20 km) northwest of the center but worth the trip for wooded slopes dotted with pavilions *(see p99)*.

5 Olympic Forest Park
Subway: Forest Park
A 1,680-acre (680-hectare) green space, Beijing's largest park *(see p44)* is due north of the Olympic venues.

6 Jing Shan Park
A hilly park *(see p71)* with a pavilion providing views of the roofscape of the Forbidden City to the south.

7 Long Tan Park
MAP G6 ▪ Subway: Tian Tan Dong Men
Lots of lakes, a kids' amusement park, and an enchanting water-screen show.

8 Ri Tan Park
One of Beijing's oldest parks, *(see p91)* featuring an altar for imperial sacrifice.

9 Temple of Heaven Park
This park *(see p16)* houses several historic structures and a vast expanse of well-tended gardens, including a rose garden.

10 Zhong Shan Park
Just outside the walls of the Forbidden City, Zhong Shan *(see p71)* offers a respite from the crowds.

Flying kites in a Beijing park

Beijing Opera

Preparing for the role of Monkey King

these characters have the most striking look of all the performers, they also usually have predominantly forceful personalities.

1 The Monkey King (Sun Wukong)

Clever, resourceful, and brave, the Monkey King is a favorite character in Beijing Opera. He has his origins in Chinese folklore, but was made famous by Wu Cheng'en's 16th-century classical novel *Journey to the West*.

2 Jing

There are four main role types in Beijing Opera: *sheng* (male), *dan* (female), *jing* (painted face), and *chou* (clown). *Jing* have stylized patterned, colored faces, and represent warriors, heroes, statesmen, adventurers, and demons. Not only do

Jing performers on stage

3 Dan

Dan are the female roles. *Laodan* are old ladies, *caidan* are female comedians, and *wudan* are martial artists. The most important category, *qingyi*, play respectable and decent ladies in elegant costumes.

4 Sheng

Sheng are divided into *laosheng*, who wear beards and represent old men, *xiaosheng* who are young men, and *wusheng*, who are acrobats.

5 Chou

The *chou* are the comic roles, characterized by white patches on their noses. Patches of different shape and size imply roles of different characters. It is the *chou* who keep the audience laughing.

The comic *chou* character

6 Mei Lanfang

The foremost male interpreter of the female role (*dan*) during Beijing Opera's heyday in the

1920s and 1930s was Mei Lanfang. All female roles were once played by male actors. However, this is no longer the case today.

7 Colors
The colors of the performers' painted faces symbolize various qualities. Red, for example, stands for loyalty and courage, purple for solemnity and a sense of justice, and green for bravery and irascibility.

Women playing the *erhu* violin

8 Musical instruments
Despite the dramatic visual elements of Beijing Opera, the Chinese say that they go to "listen" to opera, not to see it. Typically six or seven musicians accompany the dramatics. The stringed instruments usually include the *erhu*, or Chinese two-stringed violin, while percussion includes clappers, gongs, and drums.

9 Acrobatics
Beijing Opera is a form of "total theater" with singing, speech, mime, and acrobatics that combine graceful gymnastics and martial arts movements. Training is notoriously hard. Costumes are designed to make the jumps seem more spectacular by billowing out as they spin.

10 Repertoire
The traditional repertoire includes more than 1,000 works, mostly based on popular tales. Modern productions aimed at tourists often include English-language displays of the text.

TOP 10 BEIJING OPERA VENUES

Show at Huguang Guild Hall

1 Huguang Guild Hall
MAP D5 ■ 3 Hufang Lu ■ 8355 1680
One-hour highlights shows held on most days at this historic venue.

2 Chang'an Grand Theater
MAP G4 ■ 7 Jianguo Men Nei Dajie ■ www.changandaxiyuan.cn
Regular two-hour performances of mostly complete operas.

3 Mei Lanfang Grand Theater
32 Ping'Anli Xi Dajie ■ www.bjmlfdjy.cn
A prestigious theater company.

4 Tianqiao Performing Arts Center
MAP E6 ■ Building 9, Tianqiao Nandajie, Xicheng District ■ 400 635 3355
A massive arts venue specializing in ballet, musical theater and traditional opera.

5 National Center of Performing Arts
Beijing's temple to the arts offers large-scale performances (see p70).

6 Lao She Teahouse
MAP L6 ■ 3 Qian Men Xi Dajie ■ 6303 6830 ■ www.laosheteahouse.com
Daily 90-minute variety shows.

7 Tianleyuan Theatre
MAP E5 ■ 68 Xianyukou Jie ■ 139 1010 4575
Modern theater built in traditional teahouse style.

8 Mansion of Prince Gong
Summer performances only (see p27).

9 Forbidden City Concert Hall
MAP L4 ■ West Chang'an Avenue, Zhong Shan Park ■ 6559 8285
Concert venue holding occasional opera performances.

10 Zheng Yi Ci Theater
MAP K6 ■ 220 Xiheyan Qian Men ■ 138 0106 7568
Performances and 90-minute highlights shows held on selected days of the week.

🔟 Traditional Dishes

1 Thousand-year-old Eggs

These raw duck eggs are put into mud, chalk, and ammonia and left, not for 1,000 years, but several weeks. When retrieved, the yolk and white both appear darker in color. The eggs are either sprinkled with soy sauce and sesame oil, or served in rice porridge.

2 Hot Pot

Introduced to Beijing in the 13th century by the Mongols, hot pot is a much-loved staple. Hundreds of restaurants across the city sell this dish. Everybody sits around a large bubbling pot of broth dropping in their own shavings of meat, noodles, and vegetables to cook.

Whole roasted Beijing duck

Mongolian fire hot pot

3 Zha Jiang Mian

The name means "clanging dish noodles" – like hot pot, ingredients are added at the table to a central tureen of noodles, and the bowls are loudly clanged together as each dish goes in, hence the name.

4 Beijing Duck

This is arguably one of the best-known dishes in north Chinese cuisine. The duck, a local Beijing variety, is dried and brushed with a sweet marinade before being roasted over fragrant wood chips. It is carved by the chef and then eaten wrapped in pancakes with slivered scallions (spring onions) and cucumber.

5 La Mian

Watching a cook make *la mian* (hand-pulled noodles) is almost as enjoyable as eating them. First the dough is stretched and then swung like a skipping rope, so that it becomes plaited. The process is repeated several times, until the strands of dough are as thin as string.

6 Sweet and Sour Carp

Beijing cooking is heavily influenced by the cuisine of Shandong Province, generally regarded as the oldest and most traditional in China. Sweet and sour carp is a quintessential Shandong dish made with fish from the Yellow River.

Zha jiang mian

Stir-fried Kidney Flowers

These are pork kidneys cut in a criss-cross fashion and stir-fried, during which they open out like "flowers." The kidneys are typically prepared with bamboo shoots, water chestnuts, and edible black fungus.

Drunken Empress Chicken

This dish is supposedly named for Yang Guifei, an imperial concubine who was overly fond of her alcohol. The dish is prepared using Chinese wine and is served cold.

Steamer stacked with various dumplings

Jiaozi

Traditional Beijing dumplings are filled with pork, *bai cai* (Chinese leaf), and ginger but, in fact, fillings are endless. You can find *jiaozi* at snack shops all over the city. They are also sold on the street, either steamed or fried on a giant hot plate over a brazier.

10 Lamb and Scallions

Scallions (spring onions) are a common Beijing ingredient and in this dish they are rapidly stir-fried along with sliced lamb, garlic, and a sweet-bean paste.

TOP 10 BEIJING STREET FOODS

1 Lu da gun'r
Literally "donkeys rolling in dirt": sweet red-bean paste in a rice dough dusted with yellow soybean powder.

2 Jian bing
A Chinese savory crêpe often sold off the back of tricycles. It is a typical Beijing breakfast dish.

3 Zhima Shao bing
Small, dense bread roll flavored with sesame paste and spices, sometimes filled with braised beef.

4 Tang chao lizi
Chestnuts, roasted in sugar and hot sand and served in a paper bag. A seasonal snack appearing in autumn.

5 Hong shu
A winter specialty, these are baked sweet potatoes, often heated in ovens made from oil drums.

6 Chuan'r
In any area with lots of bars and clubs you'll find many places selling *chuan'r* (kebabs). They cost just a few *yuan* per skewer.

7 Baozi
These delicious steamed buns are cooked in bamboo baskets. Typical fillings include pork, chicken, beef, or vegetables and tofu.

8 Xia bing
Pie stuffed with various ingredients such as pork and cabbage or egg and chives.

9 You tiao
Deep-fried dough sticks, often served with hot soy milk for breakfast.

10 Tang hu lu
A skewer of candied hawthorn berries.

Skewered berries in a *tang hu lu*

🔟 Restaurants

Relaxed ambience at Mosto, an international bistro in Sanlitun

1 Mosto
A smart-casual restaurant serving contemporary classics with a South American twist, Mosto *(see p93)* is very popular due to its great lunch deals and buzzy Sanlitun location.

2 Georg
A tasteful fine dining affair curated by the eponymous Danish silverware brand *(see p85)*, Georg has a minimalist design, and highly creative tasting menus that celebrate individual ingredients.

Elegant dining at Georg

3 Din Tai Fung
24 Xinyuan Xili Middle Street ▪ **6462 4502** ▪ **¥¥**

This ever-popular chain specializes in southern Chinese dishes, particularly the light, fresh flavors of Zhejiang and Jiangsu provinces. Try the *xialong bao*, Shanghainese soup dumplings filled with pork or seafood prepared in a bamboo steamer.

4 TRB Hutong
MAP M2 ▪ **23 Shatan Beijie** ▪ **8400 2232** ▪ **Subway: Dong Si Shi Tiao** ▪ **¥¥¥**

Located in a beautifully restored 600-year-old temple complex, this upmarket restaurant offers superb European cuisine and a long wine list. A second TRB branch is located beside the moat of the Forbidden City *(see p73)*. Booking required.

5 Toast at the Orchid
The Orchid gained fame as a stylish hotel in the heart of a lively *hutong*, but the Middle Eastern-inspired mezze and tapas menu at its in-house restaurant *(see p85)* also has patrons raving. Come for dinner, stay for a drink, and soak up the atmosphere.

6 Lost Heaven
Located in the former US embassy compound, this restaurant *(see p79)* serves fragrant, traditional dishes from the southwestern province of Yunnan. Expect delicious delights served with edible flowers, rare mushrooms, and even Yunanese goat cheese.

7 Siji Minfu

A temple to the art of roasting, this branch (see p73) of the contemporary chain is probably Beijing's best purveyor of Peking duck. It's also a great place to sample traditional Beijing desserts and other local specialties.

8 Country Kitchen

A lively restaurant with an elegant decor (see p93), Country Kitchen offers a great selection of northern Chinese dishes such as Peking duck and roast lamb with hand-pulled noodles, as well as Sichuan dishes such as fiery chicken and prawns.

9 In & Out

This restaurant (see p93), in the heart of Beijing's Sanlitun party district, serves creatively executed Yunnan dishes in a chic industrial space. "Crossing the Bridge" noodles, grilled fish with lemongrass, and Dai-style pineapple rice, are just a few items on the menu.

10 Cai Yi Xuan

With its award-winning Cantonese cuisine, Cai Yi Xuan (see p93) offers a fine dining experience. Especially popular are the dim sum, sea cucumber, abalone, and seasonal hairy crab.

Refined table setting at Cai Yi Xuan

TOP 10 CHEAP EATS

Steamed dumplings

1 Mr Shi's Dumplings
MAP E1 ▪ 88 Baochao Hutong, Gulou Donglu
MSG-free dumplings and local dishes served by English-speaking staff.

2 Ling Er Jiu Noodles
Xingfucun Zhong Lu, Sanlitun
Some of the best noodles in Beijing are served here.

3 Pingwa Sanbao
10A Xiangjunzhuang Lu
Offers hand-pulled noodles and *chuan'r* (kebabs).

4 Nanjing Impressions
Shimao Shopping Centre, 13 Gongrentiyuchang Beilu
Plump dumplings, salted duck, and other Yangtze Delta delicacies.

5 Mama de Weidao
6–110 Zhongguo Hong Jie Building, 2 Gongti Dong Lu
Home-style northern cuisine.

6 The Southern Fish
49 Gongmenkou Toutiao
The impossibly spicy Hunan food here attracts plenty of locals; reserve ahead.

7 Xian Lao Man
252 Andingmennei Dajie, Dongcheng
Hearty dumplings, both boiled and fried, and other home-cooked dishes.

8 Zhang Mama
76 Jiaodoukou Nan Dajie
This is the place for hot Sichuan snacks.

9 Wang Pangzi
Try the famous *lurou huoshao* (braised donkey meat in bread) here (see p85).

10 Crescent Moon
16 Dongsi Liutiao
Islamic vendor of Xinjiang-style flatbreads, roasted lamb, and homemade yogurt.

For a key to restaurant price ranges see p73

🔟 Bars and Pubs

Varied selection of beer on tap at the Slow Boat Brewery

1 Slow Boat Brewery
MAP H3 ■ 6 Sanlitun Nan Lu ■ 6592 5388 ■ Subway: Tuanjiehu

A seasonally updated selection of delicious beers and award-winning burgers are served at this smart but laid-back bar, run by two American expats.

2 MO Bar
MAP H2 ■ 269 Wangfujing Jie ■ 8509 8850

Part of the Mandarin Oriental hotel, this is the only cocktail bar in Beijing with views of the Forbidden City.

3 La Social
MAP H2 ■ 3rd Floor, Nali Patio, 81 Sanlitun Lu ■ 5208 6030

This is a Columbian bar with serious food options, including

Fried *arepas* at La Social

arepas (corn flatbreads with varied fillings), and excellent cocktails. The eclectic decor includes a picture of Jesus framed by yellow bulbs, velvet lampshades, and neon busts of Mao. It is closed on Sundays.

4 Mai Bar
This smartly designed cocktail bar *(see p84)* offers outdoor seating in a narrow courtyard, plus a giant silver sofa and bar chairs inside. It draws a cool *hutong* crowd, especially at weekends.

5 Nuo Yan Rice Wine
This funky warehouse bar *(see p84)* located in the north of the Forbidden City, brews its own range of excellent *mijiu* (glutinous rice wines). Order a tasting menu to help you decide which bottle to go for.

6 Arch
This bar is hidden inside a compound that was once the residence of a warlord in the early 20th century. The cocktails and the ambience at Arch *(see p84)* are as unique as the historic setting.

7 D Lounge
MAP H2 ■ Courtyard 4, Gongti Bei Lu ■ Subway: Tuanjiehu

Sanlitun's most stylish bar, D Lounge is a cathedral-like space with a live DJ on weekends and a menu of exceptionally creative gin and tonics.

8 Centro
MAP H4 ■ Kerry Center Hotel, 1 Guanghua Lu ■ 8565 2398 ■ Subway: Guomao

Set in the lobby of one of the city's upscale hotels, Centro offers live music and an expansive terrace.

9 Great Leap Brewing #6
Beijing's original craft beer brand started in the intimate *hutong* courtyard of Great Leap Brewing #6 *(see p84)*. It remains an atmospheric setting to sample locally inspired beers brewed with Chinese ingredients, such as Sichuan peppercorns.

Beers at Great Leap Brewing #6

10 Jing-A Brewpub
MAP H2 ■ B1, Lee World Bldg, Xingfucun Zhonglu ■ 6416 5195 ■ Subway: Dongsi Shitiao

Brewer of one of Beijing's most treasured homegrown craft beer brands, Jing-A Brewpub is a stylish bar with a wide range of brews, including the Airpocalypse IPA, whose price depends on the amount of air pollution in Beijing.

TOP 10 MUSIC BARS

1 Dusk Dawn Club
14 Shanlao Hutong, Dongcheng District ■ 6407 8969
Courtyard venue with trees growing through tables and regular live shows.

2 School Live Bar
53 Wudaoying Hutong, Dongcheng District ■ 6402 8881
This *hutong* venue is one of the city's best music spots.

3 Yue Space
7 Banqiao Nanxiang
A former factory space in the *hutongs*, hosting live music and cultural events.

4 Blue Note
The New York City jazz club's first branch in China *(see p72)*.

5 Dada
MAP E2 ■ Ritan International Trade Center, Chaoyang ■ 183 1108 0818
Super-hip DJ lounge and mini club import from Shanghai.

6 Tango
MAP F1 ■ 79 Hepingli Xijie ■ 6425 5677
One of Beijing's bigger music clubs, it hosts international bands and artists.

7 Modernista
A 1920s-themed jazz and piano bar *(see p84)* that also serves Spanish tapas.

8 Nugget
MAP E2 ■ 8 Andingme Huayuan Qian Xiang ■ 131 6107 0713
This eclectic *hutong* bar and live venue has its own cassette-only record label.

9 East Shore Live Jazz Cafe
A classic pure jazz venue *(see p84)* with terrific views over Hou Hai.

10 Jianghu Bar
MAP E2 ■ 7 Dongmianhua Hutong, Jiaodaokou Nan Dajie ■ 185 1902 6150
Cozy courtyard bar hosting jam sessions.

Jianghu Bar's rustic interior

📻 **Markets and Shops**

Pearls at Hong Qiao Market

1 Hong Qiao Market

Hong Qiao (see p78) is best known for pearls (hence its alternative name, the "Pearl Market"), with a huge range of freshwater and seawater ones available on the third floor. The floors below are a tight compress of clothing, shoes, electronics, and more. Try the handy food court in the basement when visiting the nearby Temple of Heaven.

2 Parkview Green

Set within an ecologically friendly glass pyramid, this remarkable shopping mall (see p92) is strewn with quirky art installations that add a twist to its retinue of upscale boutiques and chain stores. It's also an excellent place for dining, with restaurants serving everything from fine Italian cuisine to Peking duck.

3 UCCA Store

Located inside the UCCA gallery (see p31) in the heart of the 798 Art District, this meticulously curated art shop sells designer cutting-edge objects and curios. There are also limited-edition artworks authorized and signed by featured Chinese contemporary artists.

4 Plastered T-Shirts

MAP E2 ▪ 61 Nan Luogu Xiang, Dongcheng District ▪ 6406 4872 ▪ Open 9:30am–11pm daily
A great place for gifts, Plastered offers quirky Beijing style in the form of T-shirts and tote bags. Founder Dominic Johnson Hill works with Chinese designers, and everything is manufactured in the capital. There is another shop in Wudaoying Hutong nearby.

5 Three Stone Kite Shop

MAP K1 ▪ 25A Di'an Men Xi Dajie, Xicheng District ▪ 8404 4505 ▪ Open 9am–8pm daily
Owner and craftsman, Liu Bin, comes from a long line of kite makers, some of whom once served the royal family. His kites are true works of art. Sturdy enough for Beijing breezes, they also make for exquisite, lightweight gifts. The shop runs kite-making classes, too.

Taikoo Li Sanlitun shopping center

8 Cathay Bookshop (Zhongguo Shudian)
Liulichang Xi Jie ▪ 6317 3805
▪ Open 9am–5pm daily
A bookstore with a vast selection of modern Chinese art books, as well as classic second-hand, vintage, and antique collections.

9 Beijing Postcards
97 Yangmeizhuxiejie ▪ 156
1145 3992 ▪ www.bjpostcards.com
This fascinating shop sells historic Beijing postcards, maps, calendars, and prints from the 1870s–1940s, all purchased at auction or from descendants of missionaries. See the website for information on their lectures and historical walking tours.

Colorful fabrics at the Silk Market

6 Taikoo Li Sanlitun
This hip shopping, dining, and entertainment center *(see p92)* in Sanlitun has numerous colored glass buildings housing over 200 stores, including global brand flagships such as the Apple Store and Nike, plus some of downtown Beijing's best bars and cafés.

7 Panjiayuan Antique Market
As much a tourist attraction as a shopping experience, Panjiayuan *(see p78)* is home to around 3,000 dealers peddling everything from broken bicycles to family heirlooms. Come here for Mao memorabilia, a Qing-dynasty vase, or Tintin comics in Chinese. Panjiayuan Market is at its busiest and best on weekends. Serious collectors swoop at dawn, but it's fun any time of the day.

10 Silk Market
Properly known as Xiushui, this market *(see p92)* is reportedly one the city's most popular tourist attractions, after the Forbidden City and the Great Wall. The bargains are not what they used to be and haggling is mandatory to get a good price.

Antiques on display at Panjiayuan

Beijing for Free

1 Museums

Many of Beijing's big national museums – including the Natural History Museum (see p77), the National Museum of China (see p70), and the National Art Museum of China (see p70) – offer free entry, although it is mandatory to show your passport. The Capital Museum (see p94) is free but requires you to make an online reservation before you visit.

2 Former Residence of Lao She

MAP M3 ▪ 19 Fengfu Lane, Dengshikou Xije, Dongcheng District ▪ 6514 2612 ▪ Subway: Fuchengmen ▪ Open 9am–4pm Tue–Sun

This renovated courtyard home, with an attached museum, honors Beijing personality and Chinese luminary Lao She, author of such literary classics as *Teahouse* and *Rickshaw Boy*.

3 Beijing University Campus

5 Yiheyuan Road, Haidian District ▪ 0506 5075 ▪ Subway: Peking University (East Gate)

Known locally as PKU (Peking University), Beijing University is a sprawling campus, complete with a willow-lined lake. It also features Haidian's best theater venue.

Leafy grounds at Beijing University Campus

4 Southern Moat and Central Axis

MAP E6 (Southern Moat) ▪ Access to Southern Moat via Yongdingmen Gate ▪ Access to Central Axis via Yonghe Gong Park

Beijing's once-extensive moat network has been diminished by centuries of war, structural changes, and a drying climate. Still, walking the footpath along the Forbidden City's Southern Moat is a peaceful trip back to the old city.

5 Panjiayuan Antique Market

Once called the "dirt market," when farmers used to literally unearth treasures and bring them here to sell, today Panjiayuan (see p78) is where you'll find all sorts of curios, from carved furniture to propaganda art and Qing-dynasty pottery.

Statuary at Panjiayuan Antique Market

6 Chairman Mao Memorial Hall

Visit the final resting place of Mao Zedong, built after his death in 1976, on Tian'an Men Square (see p19). The embalmed corpse of Chairman Mao is preserved in the central hall of the memorial, which is also known as the Mausoleum of Mao Zedong.

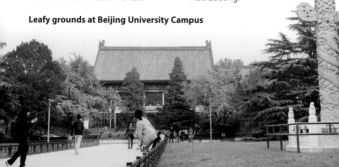

Charming Beijing *hutong*

7 Hutongs

Although they're disappearing fast due to redevelopment, *hutongs*, or traditional lanes, are where visitors will find Beijing's old-world charm. Try the side alleys off busy Nanluoguxiang and Beiluoguxiang *hutongs*, near Gulou; Wudaoying *hutong*, across from the Lama Temple; and Dashilan *hutong* in the Qian Men area.

8 Street Dancing

The so-called "dancing grannies" are senior citizens who meet in public squares for socializing and getting light exercise through activities such as fan and ballroom dancing, drumming, or low-key aerobics. This is one of Beijing's more charming features.

9 798 Art District

Many of the galleries, including one or two major international spaces, are free to enter in the 798 Art District (see pp30–31). Equally free is the street art in the form of bold murals and sculptures, scattered all over the former factory site.

10 Maliandao (Tea Street)

There's little charm about Maliandao (see p78), which is basically a tea mall for whole-salers. However, here you can see, smell, and learn everything you ever wanted to know about tea. There's an impressive range of flower types, and you can enjoy unlimited free samples.

TOP 10 BUDGET TIPS

1 Tickets
Research museums and other sights online to decide which to visit. For some sights, you can buy an all-access pass or a single-zone pass.

2 Connections
Every café has free Wi-Fi, and WeChat offers free international texts, voice messages, and phone calls.

3 Airport Transit
Both of Beijing's airports have an airport express train (one-way fare ¥25) that links up with Beijing's subway system.

4 Street Food
Eating delicious *chuan'r* (roasted kebabs) or a steaming bowl of noodles paired with a ¥5 local beer will be a highlight of your stay in Beijing.

5 Coffee Break
For a well-priced, freshly brewed cup of coffee, head to one of the 7-Eleven stores.

6 Public Spectacle
Dancing or doing tai chi with the locals costs nothing, and the experience will create a priceless memory.

7 Self-Restraint
Markets are exercises in bargaining, but the best deals come before closing time, so be sure to pace yourself.

8 Tsingtao
A bottle of Chinese beer, such as Tsingtao, is much cheaper (and larger) in a restaurant than served in a bar.

9 Two-Wheelers
Ask a local to help you rent out one of Beijing's many thousands of shared dockless bicycles.

10 Public Transport
Forget taxis; the Beijing subway costs start from ¥6. A Yikatong Card offers a 50 per cent discount on bus fares.

Rack of public bicycles

TOP 10 Festivals and Events

Fireworks and traditional dances heralding Chinese New Year

1 Chinese New Year
Three days from the 1st day of the 1st moon, usually late Jan or early Feb

Also known as Spring Festival, Beijing's major holiday ushers in temple fairs with stilt-walkers, acrobats, and fortune-tellers. Families make *jiaozi* (dumplings) together and exchange gifts, then the adults watch the annual Spring Festival Gala on television. There are no fireworks any longer as they have been banned from the capital since 2018.

2 Lantern Festival
The 15th day of the lunar calendar (end of Feb)

This festival marks the end of the 15-day Spring Festival celebrations. You might see lanterns bearing auspicious characters or in the shape of animals. It is also a time for eating the sticky rice balls – *yuanxiao*.

Decorative Lantern

3 Tomb-Sweeping Festival (Qing Ming)
Apr 5, but Apr 4 in leap years

On this public holiday, Chinese families visit their ancestors' graves to tidy them up, make offerings of snacks and alcohol, and burn incense and paper money.

4 International Labor Day
May 1

Labor Day is celebrated with a three-day holiday, which marks the start of the domestic travel season. Shops, offices, and other businesses close for the entire holiday, and often for a whole week. Don't plan on doing any out-of-town travel during this time.

5 Dragon Boat Festival (Duanwu Jie)
The 5th day of the 5th lunar month (early Jun)

This festival remembers the honest official, Qu Yuan, who drowned himself about 2,500 years ago, after banishment from the court of the Duke of Chu. Citizens threw rice cakes into the water to distract the fish from nibbling on his body, hence the wholesale consumption of these delicacies on this date. Drums thunder as dragon-headed craft compete for top honors.

Dragon Boat Festival competition

6 Chinese Valentine's Day
The 7th day of the 7th lunar month (usually Aug)

This festival celebrates the forbidden love between a mortal and a goddess. Couples exchange gifts, and single women take fruit or flowers to a temple and pray for love.

7 Mid-Autumn Festival
The 15th day of the 8th lunar month (usually Sep)

Also known as the Harvest or Moon Festival, this is traditionally a time for family reunions and for gifting sweet and savory mooncakes *(yuebing)*.

8 National Day
Oct 1

On certain anniversary years of the foundation of the People's Republic, large military parades take place along the main avenue of Chang'an Jie. The president of China inspects the troops at this televised event.

National Day on Tian'an Men Square

9 Hairy Crab Season
Oct to early Dec

This is a two-month celebration of China's favorite winter delicacy, hairy crabs, which are in season during the ninth and tenth months of the Chinese lunar calendar. Prized for their creamy meat, these are served in packed restaurants across the city.

10 Christmas Day
Dec 25

Not a traditional Chinese holiday but hotels and shopping malls put up Christmas trees, and festive parties take place in bars and restaurants.

TOP 10 CULTURAL EVENTS

1 Temple Fairs
Jan/Feb
Street fairs at several temples and parks during Chinese New Year.

2 Longqing Gorge Ice and Snow Festival
MAP G5 = Longqing Gorge = Jan & Feb
Showcases giant ice and snow sculptures illuminated by pretty colored lights in a rural setting 25 miles (40 km) northwest of Beijing *(see p105)*.

3 Beijing Auto Show
Biennial, Apr
One of the world's largest auto market.

4 Meet in Beijing Festival
Apr–Jun
A festival of theater, dance, and music by groups from several continents.

5 Art Beijing
National Agricultural Exhibition Center = May
Contemporary art fair with exhibitors from around the globe.

6 Croisements Festival
May–Jun
Festival blending French and Chinese culture, often on the same stage.

7 NLGX Performing Arts Festival
Jun–Aug
International players perform in venues in Nan Luogu Xiang *(see p81)*.

8 Beijing Dance Festival
Jul
Established modern dance companies perform alongside emerging talent.

9 Beijing International Film Festival
Various venues = Aug
This is China's largest film festival.

10 Beijing Music Festival (BMF)
Oct
Around 30, mostly classical and jazz, concerts across the city.

Opera, Meet in Beijing Festival

Beijing
Area by Area

High-rises reflected on the water in Beijing's Central Business District

🔟 Tian'an Men Square and the Forbidden City Area

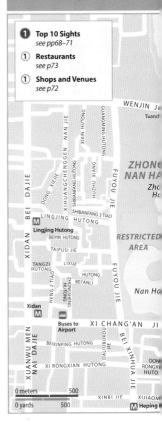

The geographical, spiritual, and historical heart of Beijing, Tian'an Men Square and the Forbidden City together represent a yin and yang arrangement; one is a vast public space, the other is an even larger walled enclosure. One represents China after the formation of the People's Republic, while the other is a silent repository of ancient imperial glories. Set aside a whole day for each. Afterward, wander around for a look at the National Center for the Performing Arts and a glimpse of the China of the future.

Vase at the National Museum of China

1 Tian'an Men Square

Although now synonymous with Beijing, until relatively recently Tian'an Men Square *(see pp18–19)* occupied a considerably smaller footprint in front of the Gate of Heavenly Peace (Tian'an Men). Cleared in the first half of the 20th century, the area quadrupled in size in 1959, supposedly allowing for up to one million people to gather. Many of the Soviet-style buildings around the square were erected at this time.

The vast Great Hall of the People

2 Great Hall of the People

MAP L5 ■ West side of Tian'an Men Square ■ 6309 6156 ■ Subway: Tian'an Men West ■ Opening hours vary ■ Adm

This is the parliament building, home of China's legislative body, the National People's Congress. Tours visit the banquet room and the 10,000-seat auditorium, with its ceiling inset with a massive red star. The building is closed to the public when the Congress is in session.

WENJIN J
Tuanch

GUANGANG HUTONG

ZHON
NAN HA
Zho
He

XIXIN HUTONG

NAN JIE

HUZHI XIANG

FUYOU JIE

XIHUANGCHENGGEN

SHIBANFANG HUTONG

DONG XIEJIE

SHIBANFANG 3 TIAO

BEI DAJIE

LINGJING HUTONG

Ⓜ Lingjing Hutong

XIDAN

BEIYIN HUTONG

TAIPUSI JIE

RESTRICTED
AREA

TANGZI
HUTONG

LIXUE

HUTONG

ZHONGSHENG'AN

HENG 2 TIAO

BEI'ANLI

FUYOU JIE

Nan Ha

Xidan
Ⓜ

Buses to
Airport

XI CHANG'AN JI

BEIXINPING HUTONG

DALIUSHUJING

XUANWU MEN
NAI DAJIE

XI RONGXIAN HUTONG

BEI XINHUA JIE

DON
RONGXI
HUTO

0 meters   500

0 yards   500

XINBI JIE   XIJIAOM

Ⓜ Heping

3 Forbidden City

The Forbidden City is Beijing's top "must-see" sight *(see pp12–15)*. A seemingly endless collection of pavilions, gates, courts, and gardens, this majestic complex encompasses five centuries of colorful – and occasionally lurid – imperial history. The palace was home to 24 emperors along with their families, concubines, and eunuch servants. Trying to see everything in one go will bring on a severe case of Ming fatigue, and it is highly recommended that you tackle this wonderful palace over at least two separate visits.

Bronze lion at the Forbidden City

TIAN'AN MEN SQUARE AND THE FORBIDDEN CITY AREA

4 Imperial City Art Museum

MAP M5 ▪ 9 Changpu Heyan
▪ 8511 5114 ▪ Subway: Tian'an Men
East ▪ Open 10am–4pm Tue–Sun
▪ Adm ▪ Audio tour available for a fee

Much of Beijing's Imperial City was
destroyed under the Communists.
A model in this museum shows just
how much has been lost, including
the wall that once encircled the city
and many temples. There are also
collections of armor and ceramics.

Fountain at Wangfujing Dajie

5 Wangfujing Dajie

MAP N4 ▪ Subway: Wangfujing

One of downtown Beijing's most
famous shopping precincts,
Wangfujing Dajie is filled with
department stores, restaurants,
and malls (see p72), as well as
several bookshops and stores selling
silk, tea, and shoes. To the north is
St. Joseph's, one of the city's most
important churches (see p42).

6 National Art Museum of China

MAP M2 ▪ 1 Wusi Dajie ▪ 8403
3500 ▪ Subway: Dong Si Shi Tiao
▪ Open 9am–5pm Tue–Sun
▪ Audio guides available for a fee
▪ www.namoc.org

This large, state-run art gallery
was erected in 1959 and built in a
style that combines Chinese and

> **THE CULT OF MAO**
>
> Mao Zedong was an ideologue whose
> impatience at the pace of reform often
> brought disaster, yet skillful maneuvering
> by the Party meant that he remained a
> heroic figure. Mao's status diminished in
> the years after his death as his influence
> was overshadowed by the political and
> economic reforms carried out by Deng
> Xiaoping and other leaders.

Socialist elements. Its 14 halls,
spread over three floors, host a
constant rotation of temporary
exhibitions of Chinese and international art.

7 National Museum of China

MAP M5 ▪ East side of Tian'an Men
Square ▪ 6511 6400 ▪ Subway:
Tian'an Men East ▪ Open 9am–5pm
Tue–Sun ▪ www.chnmuseum.cn

Combining the original Museum of
Chinese History and the Museum
of the Revolution, this huge space
offers an unsurpassed collection of
Chinese artworks and other historical,
archaeological, and cultural objects.
There are also models, documents,
and photographs connected with
the history of the Chinese
Communist Party – for political
enthusiasts only. The museum
also hosts temporary exhibitions.

8 National Center for the Performing Arts

MAP K5 ▪ 2 West Chang An Jie
▪ 6655 0000 ▪ Subway: Tian'an Men
West ▪ www.chncpa.org

This modern opera house, a major
landmark on Beijing's skyline, hosts a
year-round program of opera, theater,
and concerts. Designed by French
architect Paul Andreu, it is built of

National Center for the Performing Arts

glass and titanium and takes the form of a giant parabolic dome – earning it the nickname "The Egg." Entrance is through an underwater tunnel.

(9) Jing Shan Park

MAP L2 ▪ 1 Wenjin Jie ▪ 6404 4071 ▪ Subway: Shichahai ▪ Bus: 5, 111, 124 ▪ Open 6am–9pm daily (Nov–Mar: 6:30am–8pm daily) ▪ Adm

Jing Shan lies north of the Forbidden City. The hill, created from the earth that was excavated while building the moat around the palace complex, was meant to protect the emperor and his court from malign northern influences, which brought death and destruction according to *feng shui*. The park is dotted with pavilions and halls, but the highlight is the view over the Forbidden City from the hilltop Wancheng Pavilion.

View from the hill of Jing Shan Park

(10) Zhong Shan Park

MAP L4 ▪ 6605 5431 ▪ Subway: Tian'an Men West ▪ Open 6am–9pm daily ▪ Adm

Northwest of the Tian'an Men, Zong Shan (also known as Sun Yat Sen Park), the oldest public park in the city, offers respite from the crowds thronging the nearby sights. It was once part of the grounds of a temple, and the square Altar of Earth and Harvests remains. Located here is the Forbidden City Concert Hall, Beijing's premier venue for classical music.

A DAY AROUND TIAN'AN MEN SQUARE AND WANGFUJING DAJIE

▶ MORNING

Arrive early to beat the crowds at the **Chairman Mao Memorial Hall** *(see p19)* and shuffle through for the permitted few minutes in the presence of the Great Helmsman. The Forbidden City can be saved for another day, but climb the **Tian'an Men** *(see p18)* for the views from the gallery. From the gate, walk west along the Imperial City wall and into **Zhong Shan Park**. Take a walk through the park and stop by the box office to check for concert tickets before heading east to the Imperial Ancestral temple, an ancient place of worship now known as the Workers' Cultural Palace. From there, continue eastwards to **Wangfujing Dajie** and the **Oriental Plaza** mall *(see p72)*. Browse Beijing's first ritzy shopping district, then hit **Haidilao Hot Pot** *(see p73)* for lunch.

AFTERNOON

Wander up **Wangfujing Dajie**, making sure to look in the silk and tea shops. At No. 74 is the attractive **St. Joseph's Church** *(see p42)*, which is well worth a look. Immediately before the church is a crossroads: head away from the church along Deng Shi Kou Jie looking for signs for Fengfu Hutong on your right. Here is the **Former Residence of Writer Lao She** *(see p62)*, offering a glimpse into a way of life fast disappearing in Beijing. Keep heading north to **Susu** *(see p73)*, for a Vietnamese dinner in a converted courtyard.

See map on pp68–9 ←

Shops and Venues

1 Oriental Plaza
MAP N5 ■ 1 Dong Chang'an Jie

A long, narrow shopping mall of high-end, big-name international retailers, together with a food court and cinema complex.

2 Foreign Languages Bookstore
MAP N4 ■ 235 Wangfujing Dajie

Most of the first floor here is devoted to English-language fiction and non-fiction works and the staff are reliably surly.

3 Ten Fu's Tea
MAP N4 ■ 88 Wangfujing Dajie
■ www.tenfu.com

Tea from all over China is sold loose or in beautiful presentation boxes at this lovely shop. Staff will even brew small cups for sampling.

4 APM
MAP N4
■ 138 Wangfujing Dajie

This shopping mall full of mid-range clothes shops also has a multiscreen cinema as well as plenty of restaurants on the top floor.

5 Gongmei Building
MAP N4
■ 200 Wangfujing Dajie

A vast, multistory emporium of all kinds of handicrafts, from cloisonné vases and jade to wood carvings, lacquer ware, and silks.

6 Chairman Mao Memorial Hall
MAP L5 ■ Tian'an Men Square
■ Subway: Qian Men ■ Open 8:30–11:30am Mon–Sat, 2–4pm Mon, Wed & Fri

The mausoleum gift shop sells Mao badges, posters, and shoulder bags.

7 Forbidden City Concert Hall
MAP L4 ■ West Chang'an Avenue, Zhong Shan Park ■ 6559 8285

This venue draws the best musicians in town. In summer, the Gateway to Music Festival sees big names and traditional music concerts (see p53).

8 Capital Theater
MAP N4 ■ 22 Wangfujing Dajie
■ 6512 1598

The city's smartest theater plays classic Chinese dramas, plus the occasional foreign Shakespeare show, to captivated audiences.

9 Blue Note
MAP N6 ■ 23 Qianmen Dongdajie

International artists play at this classy subterranean jazz venue.

10 Yintai In88
MAP N4 ■ 88 Wangfujing Dajie

This high-end mall is jointly owned by the Korean department giant Lotte and the Chinese Yintai group. It also hosts cultural events and exhibitions.

Yintai In88

Restaurants

1 Susu
MAP M2 ■ 10 Qiangliang Xixiang, off Qianliang Hutong ■ 8400 2699 ■ ¥¥

Susu serves light Vietnamese fare, including spring rolls. The English-speaking staff can turn meat dishes into vegetarian options. Book ahead.

2 Dong Lai Shun
MAP N4 ■ 198 Wangfujing Dajie ■ 6513 9661 ■ ¥¥

An old name well-known for Mongolian-style hot pots. Get plates of sliced meat and vegetables to cook your own meal in a copper-funneled pot.

Oriental Plaza Food Court

3 Oriental Plaza Food Court
MAP N4 ■ Corner of Dong Chang'an Jie and Wangfujing Dajie ■ ¥

The basement of this upscale shopping mall has a Southeast Asian-style food court offering everything from good Chinese street food to sushi.

4 Made In China
MAP N5 ■ Grand Hyatt, 1 Dong Chang'an Jie ■ 6510 9608 ■ ¥¥¥

A classy venture known for its traditional Peking duck and northern Chinese dishes.

5 Jing
MAP N4 ■ The Peninsula Beijing Hotel, 8 Jinyu Hutong ■ 8516 2888 (ext 6758) ■ ¥¥¥

Enjoy an outstanding Asian-flavored French menu in refined surrounds.

PRICE CATEGORIES
For the equivalent of a meal for two made up of a range of dishes, served with two glasses of wine, and including service.

¥ under ¥250   ¥¥ ¥250–¥500
¥¥¥ over ¥500

6 TRB Forbidden City
95 Donghuamen Dajie, Dongcheng District ■ 6401 6676 ■ ¥¥¥

One of Beijing's top restaurants shows its more casual side, but its pedigree shines through. Choose from around 20 selections to customize your three to five courses. Another TRB branch is located at Shatan Beijie, Dongcheng District *(see p56)*.

7 Haidilao Hot Pot
MAP N4 ■ 8th Floor, Yintai In88, 88 Wangfujing Dajie ■ 5762 0153 ■ ¥¥

Try their delicious hotpot and friendly service. Get your shoes shined, or have a manicure while you wait.

8 Quanjude
MAP N5 ■ 9 Shuai Fu Yuan Hutong, Wangfujing Dajie ■ 6525 3310 ■ ¥¥

Beijing's famous duck restaurant has several branches but this is definitely the most convenient, just a short walk from southern Wangfujing.

9 Siji Minfu
11 Nanchizi Dajie ■ 6526 7369 ■ ¥¥

Enjoy perfect Peking duck in this hugely popular restaurant with a terrace overlooking the Forbidden City's moat. If it's too busy there is another branch nearby at 53 Donghuamen Dajie.

10 Huang Ting
MAP N4 ■ The Peninsula Beijing Hotel, 8 Jinyu Hutong ■ 8516 2888 (ext 6757) ■ ¥¥

Enjoy Cantonese cuisine amid splendid antique furniture in the basement of a five-star hotel.

See map on pp68–9

🔟 South of Tian'an Men Square

The Qian Men (Front Gate) at the southern end of Tian'an Men Square was once part of the inner walls that divided the imperial quarters from the "Chinese city," where the massed populace lived. Walking south from the gate you reach Qian Man Dajie, a restored shopping street, with a network of historic *hutongs* to the west. Continuing south beyond Qian Men Dajie brings you to the western perimeter of the Temple of Heaven, one of Beijing's most evocative sights.

Incense burner at Fayuan Temple

① Fayuan Temple
MAP C6 ▪ 7 Fayuan Si Qian Jie ▪ 6353 4171 ▪ Subway: Caishikou, then a 10-minute walk ▪ Open 8:30am–3:30pm daily ▪ Adm

Dating from AD 696, this is most likely the oldest temple in Beijing. Near the gate, the incense burner is flanked by the Drum and Bell Towers. Beyond, the Hall of the Heavenly Kings is guarded by a pair of bronze lions. A hall contains a large statue of Buddha.

SOUTH OF TIAN'AN MEN SQUARE

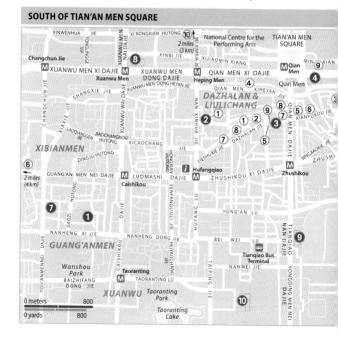

Colorful building in Liulichang

a gathering spot for writers, artists, and musicians, Liulichang takes its name from the glazed tile factory once located here. The streets are lined with shops selling Chinese paintings, musical instruments, porcelain, and calligraphy – look out for the giant ink brushes hanging in the windows. During Chinese New Year, Liulichang is home to one of Beijing's most colorful Temple Fairs.

② Liulichang
MAP D5 ■ Subway: Heping Men

Head west from the bustle of Qian Men and Dazhalan into a more peaceful *hutong* district. Historically

③ Qian Men and Dazhalan
MAP D5–E5 ■ Subway: Qian Men

A historical royal street as well as a traditional shopping area, Qian Men Dajie has been redeveloped into a period-themed shopping boulevard replete with a faux-1920s tram and birdcage-like streetlamps. Running west off the northern end of Qian Men is Dazhalan Jie, or Dashilan, an old *hutong* area that can be explored on foot or by rickshaw. It is full of Qing-era specialty shops selling pickles, tea, silks, as well as traditional Chinese medicine.

④ Beijing Planning Exhibition Hall
MAP L6 ■ 20 Qian Men Dong Dajie ■ 6701 7074 ■ Subway: Qian Men ■ Open 9am–5pm Tue–Sun (passport required for entry) ■ www.bjghzl.com.cn

On display at this four-floor museum are dreams of the architecture and urban landscape of Beijing to be. These are dramatically represented through film and interactive exhibits, plus a vast model that covers most of the third floor.

Beijing Planning Exhibition Hall

5 Legation Quarter
MAP M5 ▪ Subway: Qian Men

At the end of the Second Opium War, in 1860, foreign delegations were permitted to take up residence in a quarter southeast of the Forbidden City. On Dong Jiao Min Xiang and the surrounding streets, the first modern foreign buildings in Beijing took root. The embassies have long since left, and new occupants have moved in. The former American legation, for instance, now hosts, among others, a Yunnan restaurant and a jazz club. Also here are the former City Bank of New York, now the Beijing Police Museum *(see p40)*, and St. Michael's Church *(see p43)*.

THE BOXERS

The Boxers, a band of xenophobic rebels from north China who rose up to rid China of the "foreign devils," drew from superstitious rituals that they believed made them invulnerable. Supported by the Empress Dowager Cixi *(see p29)*, the rebels laid waste to Beijing's Legation Quarter in 1900 while besieging the district's foreign population. The siege was eventually broken by an eight-power allied force.

6 Temple of Heaven

The name refers to a vast complex that encompasses a large, marble sacrificial altar, the iconic three-story Hall of Prayer for Good Harvests, the smaller Imperial Vault of Heaven, and many ancillary buildings, all set in a landscaped park. Allow at least a half-day to take in everything *(see pp16–17)*.

Ornate hall in the Temple of Heaven

Looking inside Niu Jie Mosque

7 Niu Jie Mosque
MAP C6 ▪ 88 Niu Jie ▪ 6353 2564 ▪ Subway: Guanganmennei, then walk ▪ Open 8am–sunset daily ▪ Adm

Beijing's oldest and largest mosque dates back to the 10th century. It's an attractive building with Islamic motifs and Arabic verses decorating its halls. Astronomical observations were made from the tower-like Wangyue Lou. The lush courtyard is an idyllic escape from the city streets. Visitors should dress conservatively, and non-Muslims are not allowed to enter the prayer hall.

8 South Cathedral
MAP J6 ▪ 141 Qian Men Xi Dajie ▪ Subway: Xuanwu Men ▪ English Mass: 10:30am Sun

Known officially in Beijing as the Cathedral of the Immaculate Conception, this was the first Catholic church to be built in the city. It stands on the site of the residence of the first Jesuit missionary to reach the city, Matteo Ricci. Arriving in 1601, the Italian won the favor of the Wanli emperor by presenting him with gifts of European curiosities such as mathematical instruments and clocks. Ricci founded the church in 1605, although the present building dates to 1904, replacing a structure that was burned down during the Boxer Rebellion. It has some fine stained-glass windows.

(9) Natural History Museum

MAP E6 ■ 126 Tangqiao Nan Dajie ■ 6702 7702 ■ Subway: Zhushikou, then walk ■ Open 9am–5pm Tue–Sun ■ www.bmnh.org.cn

This overbearing piece of 1950s architecture houses a great collection of dinosaur skeletons, as well as stuffed pandas and other animals. There are also fish, both dead (preserved in formaldehyde) and alive (in the aquarium).

Ancient Architecture Museum

(10) Ancient Architecture Museum

MAP D6 ■ 21 Dongjing Lu ■ 6304 5608 ■ Bus 15 to Nanwei Lu ■ Open 9am–4pm Tue–Sun ■ Adm (audio guide ¥10, plus ¥100 deposit)

Housed in the Hall of Jupiter, part of the Xiannong Tan temple complex, this museum focuses on the ancient construction techniques of Beijing buildings, all illuminated with detailed models. A fascinating 3D plan shows the city as it was in 1949, its city walls and gates largely intact.

A DAY SOUTH OF TIAN'AN MEN SQUARE

▶ MORNING

Start on Tian'an Men Square, at the southeast corner beside the stripey brick Old Qian Men Railway Station, built by the British in 1906, partly to bring military forces straight to the assistance of foreigners in case of a repeat of the siege of the Boxers. It's now a **Railway Museum** *(see p18)*. Venture east along Dong Jiao Min Xiang into the **Legation Quarter** to visit the **Police Museum** *(see p40)*. On leaving, head south to Qian Men Dong Dajie and walk back west for a glimpse of the Beijing of the future at the **Beijing Planning Exhibition Hall** *(see p75)*. From the museum, head into the *hutongs* toward Dazhalan for some crispy roast duck at **Deyuan** *(see p79)*.

AFTERNOON

Head east along **Dazhalan Jie** *(see p75)*. This is a great place for specialty shops. Located down the first alley is 400-year-old **Liubiju** *(see p78)*, selling a vast array of pickles. **Ruifuxiang** *(see p78)* dates from 1893 and is renowned for silks. **Tongrentang Pharmacy** *(see p78)* has been in business since 1669, while **Zhangyiyuan Chazhuang** has been trading teas since the early 20th century. For an unconventional tea-tasting experience, head west to **Alice's Tea House** *(see p79)*, then grab dinner at the trendy and casual **Suzuki Kitchen** *(see p79)*.

See map on pp74–5 ←

Shops

Souvenir shop on Liulichang

1 Liulichang
This picturesque street *(see p75)* was renovated in the 1980s to give it an Old China look. It's still fun to browse for antiques and art supplies.

2 Hong Qiao Market
MAP F6 ▪ 36 Hong Qiao Lu ▪ 6713 3354 ▪ Open 8:30am–7pm daily
Specializing in pearls and precious stones, this indoor market also sells clothes, bags, and shoes *(see p60)*.

3 Panjiayuan Antique Market
MAP E5 ▪ Panjiayuan Qiao ▪ 6775 2405 ▪ Subway: Panjiayuan ▪ Open 8:30am–6pm Mon–Fri, 4:30am–6pm Sat & Sun
Set the alarm for dawn for a treasure hunt down at Beijing's sprawling flea market *(see p61)*.

Antiques from Panjiayuan

4 Beijing Curio City
MAP E5 ▪ 21 Dong San Huan Nan Lu ▪ 6774 7711 ▪ Subway: Panjiayuan ▪ Open 10am–7pm daily
Just south of Panjiayuan, Curio City has four levels of antiques, porcelain, carpets, Buddhist statues and jewelry.

5 Neiliansheng
MAP E5 ▪ 34 Dazhalan Jie ▪ 6301 4863
Beijing's best-known shoe store, in business since 1853 is known for supplying footwear to Chairman Mao.

6 Maliandao Tea Street
MAP B6 ▪ 11 Maliandao Lu, Guang'anmen Wai ▪ Bus 46, 89, 414, or special line 27 ▪ Open 9am–7pm daily
This three-floor market (literally, "tea street") could also be called "Little Fujian," so ubiquitous are traders from China's tea capital. It's Beijing's best place to buy or sample an incredible variety of teas.

7 Ruifuxiang
MAP E5 ▪ 5 Dazhalan Dong Jie ▪ 6303 5764 ▪ Open 9am–9pm daily
Silk has been sold on this precise spot since 1893. Tailors can create pretty blouses and *qipaos* (the old-style Chinese dress).

8 Qian Xiang Yi Silk Store
MAP E5 ▪ 5 Zhubaoshi, Qianmen Jie ▪ 6301 6658
This venerable store is said to date back to 1840. Prices for quality tailoring and ready-made clothes are reasonable.

9 Tongrentang Pharmacy
MAP E5 ▪ 24 Qian Men Dazhalan
Founded in 1669, Tongrentang is China's oldest pharmacy. The store stocks thousands of traditional medicines, some of which were used in the imperial court.

10 Liubiju
MAP E5 ▪ 3 Liangshidian Jie
A jar of Chinese pickles may not be high on your list of essentials, but a visit to this colorful, nearly 500-year-old shop should be.

See map on pp74–5

Restaurants and Teahouses

PRICE CATEGORIES

For the equivalent of a meal for two made up of a range of dishes, served with two glasses of wine, and including service.

¥ under ¥250   ¥¥ ¥250–¥500
¥¥¥ over ¥500

① Soloist Coffee Co
MAP E5 ■ 39 Yangmeizhu Xiejie, near Maishi Jie ■ 5711 1717 ■ ¥

Soloist's coffee is roasted in-house, and wait staff are friendly coffee snobs who make perfect brews.

② Suzuki Kitchen
MAP E5 ■ 16 Yangmeizhu Xie Jie, Dongcheng District ■ 6313 5409 ■ ¥

A small and cozy restaurant that serves great Japanese hotpot and curries at very reasonable prices.

③ Liqun Roast Duck Restaurant
MAP M6 ■ 11 Beixianfeng Hutong, enter via Zhengyi Lu ■ 6705 5578 ■ ¥¥

Beijing duck at this little courtyard restaurant is usually sublime, despite the rough-and-ready ambience.

④ Lao She Teahouse
MAP L6 ■ 3 Qian Men Xi Dajie ■ 6303 6830 ■ ¥¥

A fascinating old-style Beijing teahouse that hosts acrobatics and opera shows in a small upstairs theater. It's a touristy spot, but worth a visit nonetheless.

Decorative exterior, Lao She Teahouse

⑤ Qian Men Quanjude
MAP L6 ■ 32 Qian Men Dajie ■ 6511 2418 ■ ¥¥

A famous Quanjude restaurant; Call by for take-away duck pancakes.

⑥ Bianyifang Road Duck
MAP M6 ■ Xianyukou Jie ■ 6708 8680 ■ ¥¥

Said to be Beijing's oldest duck roaster, Bianyifang serves juicy roast fowl with little bread rolls called *shaobing*.

⑦ Alice's Tea House
81 Tieshuxie Jie, Xicheng District ■ 6908 0852 ■ ¥

The friendly owner, Alice, will take you through the varieties of Chinese tea and the tea ceremony. Book ahead.

⑧ Deyuan
MAP E5 ■ 57 Dashilan Xi Dajie, Xicheng District ■ 6308 5371 ■ ¥¥

One of the better places to enjoy duck with locals, not tourists – and at bargain prices, too.

⑨ Lost Heaven
MAP E4 ■ 23 Qian Men Dong Dajie ■ 8516 2698 ■ ¥¥¥

A luxuriously designed restaurant serving a tangy fusion of Yunnan, Thai, and Burmese cuisines.

⑩ Lao Beijing Zhajiang Mian Da Wang
MAP E5 ■ 56 Dong Xinglong Jie ■ 6701 1116 ■ ¥

A bustling spot selling traditional Beijing snacks. Cheap and tasty fare.

🔟 North of the Forbidden City

An almost contiguous run of lakes, either set in parkland or surrounded by charming *hutongs*, stretches through the neighborhood north of the Forbidden City. It's a rewarding area to explore on foot: along its narrow streets you'll find ancient temples and grand old courtyard residences, and the recent influx of restaurants, bars, and shops has not spoiled the picturesque setting.

Boating in Bei Hai Park

NORTH OF THE FORBIDDEN CITY

1 Top 10 Sights
see pp80–83

1 Restaurants
see p85

1 Bars
see p84

0 meters 500
0 yards 500

1 Bei Hai Park

A classic imperial garden, Bei Hai was a summer playground for successive dynasties that ruled from the neighboring Forbidden City. Now open to the public, it is thronged by locals who come here to socialize. The white *dagoba*, towering over the lake, is one of the most impressive sights in central Beijing. This is arguably the loveliest of Beijing's many fine city parks *(see pp24–5).*

2 Drum Tower

■ MAP E2 ■ Gulou Dong Dajie ■ 8403 6706 ■ Subway: Zhonglou ■ Open 8:30am–9pm daily (Nov–Mar: to 4:30pm) ■ Adm

Drum towers *(gu lou)* were once found in all major Chinese towns. They housed large drums that were beaten to mark the hour, keeping the city's civil servants on time for work. The current structure dates to 1894. Visitors can see a time-

Inside the 15th-century Drum Tower

keeping exhibition and be entertained by drummers delivering skin-thumping performances. Call ahead for performance times.

3 Bell Tower

■ MAP E1 ■ Gulou Dong Dajie ■ 8403 6706 ■ Subway: Zhonglou ■ Open 8:30am–9pm daily (Nov–Mar: to 4:30pm) ■ Adm

Dating from 1745, this replaces an earlier tower that burned down. The heavy bell it contains used to be rung to mark the closing of the city gates in the evening. These days, the bell is rung once a year on December 31st. The views from both the Drum and Bell Towers are well worth the exhausting climb.

4 Nan Luogu Xiang

■ MAP E2

Close to the Drum Tower, Nan Luogu Xiang is Beijing's most touristy *hutong*, with shops selling snacks and souvenirs. There are a number of cafés and bars here. The real interest is to wander along the much quieter *hutongs* that cross Nan Luogu Xiang.

Boutique in Nan Luogu Xiang

CONFUCIUS

Born during an age of war, Confucius (551–479 BC) was prompted by the suffering around him to develop a philosophy built on the principle of virtue. Finding no audience among his native rulers, he set off in search of a ruler who would apply his rules of governance. He never found such a person and died unrecognized.

5 Xu Beihong Memorial Museum

MAP D1 ■ 53 Xinjiekou Bei Dajie ■ 6225 2187 ■ Subway: Jishuitan ■ Open 9am–4pm Tue–Sun ■ Adm (audio guide ¥10, plus ¥100 deposit)

Considerably expanded in 2019, this museum is dedicated to the man regarded as the founder of modern Chinese painting. It exhibits a collection of the lively watercolors of horses that made Xu Beihong (1885–1953) inter-nationally famous.

Statue at the Confucius Temple

6 Lama Temple (Yonghe Gong)

About a 30-minute walk east of the Drum and Bell Towers, or just a few minutes south of the Yonghe Gong subway station, the Lama Temple (see pp20–21) is Beijing's largest working temple complex. It is filled every day with both visitors and worshipers.

7 Confucius Temple (Kong Miao)

MAP F1 ■ 13 Guozi Jian Jie ■ 8402 7224 ■ Subway: Yonghe Gong ■ Open 8:30am–5pm daily ■ Adm

Located to the west of the Lama Temple, the Confucius Temple was built in 1302 during the Mongol Yuan dynasty, and expanded in 1906. Around 200 ancient stelae stand in the courtyard in front of the main hall, inscribed with the names of those who successfully passed the imperial civil service exams. On a marble terrace inside the hall are statues of Confucius and a number of his disciples.

8 Hou Hai

One of Beijing's most popular neighborhoods, Hou Hai (see pp26–7) consists of three joined lakes surrounded by an expansive and labyrinthine sprawl of age-old *hutongs* (alleys). Visit to admire a

Red-and-gold pavilion at the Lama Temple (Yonghegong)

Willow-lined lake in Hou Hai

handful of well-preserved mansions, as well as for the opportunity to see a more humble form of Beijing life as it has been lived for centuries.

9 Former Residence of Mei Lanfang

MAP D2 ▪ 9 Huguosi Jie ▪ 8322 3598 ▪ Subway: Jishuitan ▪ Open 9am–4pm Tue–Sun ▪ Adm ▪ www.meilanfang.com.cn

This was the home of Beijing Opera's greatest ever performer (1894–1961). The rear rooms have been left with their traditional furniture as it was when he died. Others contain a hagiographic account of his life, as well as diagrams of the stylized movements required by the form, and a video of Mei, aged 61 but still playing the young girl roles for which he was famous (see p52).

10 Di Tan Park

MAP F1 ▪ North of Lama Temple ▪ Subway: Yonghe Gong ▪ Open 6am–8:30pm daily (Nov–Mar: to 9pm daily) ▪ Adm ▪ www.dtpark.com

The park was named for the Altar of Earth (Di Tan), which was a venue for imperial sacrifices. The altar's square shape represents the earth. These days, the park is always full of pensioners strolling, chatting, and exercising. A lively temple fair is held here at Chinese New Year.

A DAY IN THE HUTONGS

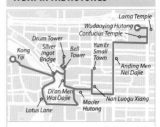

Lama Temple
Wudaoying Hutong
Confucius Temple
Drum Tower
Silver Ingot Bridge
Bell Tower
Kong Yiji
Yun Er Small Town
Anding Men Nei Dajie
Di'an Men Wai Dajie
Mao'er Hutong
Nan Luogu Xiang
Lotus Lane

▶ MORNING

Take a morning stroll along Wudaoying Hutong, where you can have breakfast at one of the cafés. Then continue on to the **Lama Temple** (see pp20–21). On leaving, cross over the main road and pass under the pailou (gate) at the entrance to Guozi Jian Jie for the **Confucius Temple**. At the western end of Guozi Jian Jie turn left onto **Anding Men Nei Dajie**, a wide, shop-filled avenue, follow it south across Jiaodaokuo Dong Dajie and take a right on Dongmianhua Hutong, one of the more vibrant of the city's old alleys. Take the first left onto **Nan Luogu Xiang** (see p81), cross Gu Lou Dong Dajie to Bei Luogu Xiang, and stop for a Yunnan lunch on the terrace of **Yun Er Small Town** (see p85) before hitting the boutiques.

AFTERNOON

Head west along **Mao'er Hutong** until you reach **Di'an Men Wai Dajie**, where you turn right and up the street for the **Drum Tower** and the **Bell Tower** (see p81). Climb the towers to see the route you've just taken. Retrace your steps back down Di'an Men Wai Dajie taking the very first right, a narrow opening (usually marked by waiting taxis) leads into Yandai Xie Jie (see p27). At the end of this crooked alley is the **Silver Ingot Bridge** (see p26); cross and bear left for **Lotus Lane** (see p27). For dinner, head west around the shore for a fine lakeside meal at **Kong Yiji** (see p57).

See map on pp80–81

Bars

Outdoor seating at Cafe Zarah

1 Cafe Zarah
MAP F1 ■ 46 Gulou Dongdajie
■ 8403 9807

A hip café by day and a cool cocktail bar after dark, Cafe Zarah is a great place to experience Gulou neighborhood's alternative and arty scenes.

2 Nuo Yan Rice Wine
MAP F2 ■ 7 Banqiao South Alley
■ 134 2628 6012

With a sophisticated air about it and a unique, expansive rice wine list, Nuo Yan has secured a place among the top bars in town. You can also learn about rice wine production here.

3 Peiping Machine
MAP F1 ■ Bldg 101, 46 Fangjia Hutong ■ 6401 1572

A local, Chinese-run craft brewery, Peiping Machine is set inside a former factory building in the *hutongs*. Along with its own brews, it serves craft beers from all over China.

4 Mao Mao Chong
MAP E2 ■ 12 Banchang Hutong, off Jiaodaokou Nanje ■ 6405 5718

A laid-back and affordable *hutong* bar, Mao Mao Chong offers a selection of creative cocktails, plus pizzas and wings. The owner is friendly and speaks English.

5 The Tiki Bungalow
MAP F2 ■ 46 Fangjia Hutong

This roomy, popular *hutong* bar brings the tropics to Beijing. There are over 60 cocktails, and the staff have an intimate knowledge of rum.

6 Modernista
MAP E1 ■ 44 Baochao Hutong
■ 136 9142 5744

Keep the winter chill at bay with the many varieties of absinthe served at this 1920s-themed jazz and piano bar *(see p59)*. In summer, try the sangria.

7 Arch
MAP F2 ■ 3 Zhangzizhong Lu
■ 6409 3319

An intimate, classy bar tucked in a corner away from the bustle of central Beijing. Enjoy the potent cocktails made from the choicest of liquors.

8 Mai Bar
MAP E1 ■ 40 Bei Luogu Xiang
■ 138 1125 2641

Visit this tiny bar *(see p58)* to choose from a wide range of cocktails prepared by a trained mixologist.

9 East Shore Live Jazz Café
MAP E2 ■ 2 Qianhai Nanyan Lu
■ 8403 2131

Opened by famous jazzman Liu Yuan, this bar has steep wooden stairs, four walls of floor-to-ceiling windows and a roof terrace, plus live music.

10 Great Leap Brewing #6
MAP E2 ■ 6 Doujiao Hutong, off Di'an Men Wai Dajie ■ 5717 1399

Located on a quiet *hutong*, this craft beer pioneer offers a pleasant courtyard and free spicy peanuts.

Restaurants

PRICE CATEGORIES
For the equivalent of a meal for two made up of a range of dishes, served with two glasses of wine, and including service.

¥ under ¥250   ¥¥ ¥250–¥500
¥¥¥ over ¥500

1 Xian Lao Man
MAP E2 ▪ 252 Andingmennei Dajie ▪ 6404 6944 ▪ ¥

Popular with locals, Xian Lao Man serves exceptionally good-value dumplings, alongside tasty favorites such as *kungpao* (sweet and savory) chicken and Beijing-style *zhajiang* (pork cubes with noodles).

2 Cafe Sambal
MAP E1 ▪ 43 Doufuchi Hutong, off Jiugulou Dajie ▪ 6400 4875 ▪ ¥¥

An old-style courtyard house serves exquisite dishes cooked by a talented and creative Malaysian chef. The focus here is on modern Malaysian cuisine, with an influence from Southeast Asia.

3 Georg
45 Dongbuyaqiao Hutong, nr Dianmen Dajie ▪ 8408 5300 ▪ ¥¥¥

Run by the Danish brand Georg Jensen, this place *(see p56)* attracts Beijing's A-list crowd. European dishes created with Scandanavian sophistication are on offer here.

4 Kaorou Ji
MAP E2 ▪ 14 Qianhai Dong Yan ▪ 6404 2554 ▪ ¥¥

This longstanding restaurant majors in Qingzhen – Hui or Muslim – cuisine, which means mutton. The specialty here is barbecued lamb, and sesame seed bread.

5 Kong Yiji
MAP E2 ▪ Desheng Men Nei Dajie ▪ 6618 4917 ▪ ¥

A lovely lakeside restaurant with a range of exquisite dishes from the Yangzi River delta.

6 Nuage
MAP E2 ▪ 22 Qian Hai Dong Yan ▪ 6401 9581 ▪ ¥

A Vietnamese restaurant with a rooftop terrace and a lovely setting just east of the Silver Ingot Bridge.

7 Yun Er Small Town
MAP E1 ▪ 84 Bei Luogu Xiang ▪ ¥

A well-priced option, Yun Er *(see p57)* has a rooftop terrace and the best Yunnan fried cheese in town.

8 Toast at the Orchid
MAP E2 ▪ 65 Baochao Hutong, Dongcheng District ▪ 8404 4818 ▪ ¥¥¥

Toast *(see p56)* has a relaxed ambience and fusion food that blends flavours of the Middle-East with those of Asia and North Africa.

9 Jin Ding Xuan
MAP D2 ▪ 77 Hepingli Xijie ▪ 6429 6699 ▪ ¥¥

Close to the entrance of Ditan Park, this 24-hour restaurant serves hearty Cantonese dim sum over three brightly lit floors.

10 Wang Pangzi
76 Gulou Xidajie ▪ 8402 3077 ▪ ¥¥

This is one of the most famous purveyors in Beijing of *luorou huoshao* – braised donkey meat in bread. It also serves cold salad dishes. It has many branches around town.

**Grill skin
Beijing duck**

See map on pp80–81 ←

🔟 Eastern Beijing

East of central Beijing is the large district of Chaoyang. It's not an area that is particularly old and it doesn't have very many significant monuments, but it is home to two main clusters of international embassies and the Central Business District, and it is where a large proportion of the city's expatriate community chooses to live. As a result, Chaoyang is the city's entertainment and nightlife center, and, for visitors, it is the prime area for shopping and international dining.

CCTV Tower, Central Business District

EASTERN BEIJING

① Top 10 Sights
see pp88–91

① Restaurants
see p93

① Shops, Markets, and Malls
see p92

5 miles (8 km)

0 kilometers 1

0 miles 1

Previous pages The Great Wall of China at Jinshanling

Courtyard of the Ancient Observatory

1 Ancient Observatory
MAP G4 ■ 6524 2202
■ Subway: Jianguo Men ■ Open
9am–5pm Tue–Sun ■ Adm

Dating to 1442, Beijing's observatory is one of the oldest in the world. In fact, there was an even earlier Yuan-dynasty (1279–1368) observatory also located on this site but no trace of that remains. Today, a collection of astronomical devices dating back to the Qing dynasty can be found on the observatory roof, some of them are decorated with fantastic Chinese designs. There are more impressive instruments on the roof.

2 Central Business District (CBD)
MAP H4 ■ Subway: Jianguo Men,
Yong'an Li, Guomao or Dawanglu

The Central Business District is Beijing's business hub, a neigh-borhood of glass and steel skyscrapers overlooking neat, orderly streets. Marked by the CCTV Tower, China Zun (Beijing's tallest skyscraper) and China World Tower 3, the area is also home to about half of the city's luxury hotels and two of its glitziest shopping malls, China World and Parkview Green (see p92).

3 Chaoyang Theater
MAP G3 ■ 36 Dongsanhuan
Beilu ■ 6507 2421 ■ Subway: Hujialou
■ Performances: 4pm, 5:30pm &
7pm daily

The home of Beijing's premier acrobatics show, Chaoyang Theater reverberates nightly with the cheers of punters enjoying feats of daring and athleticism to rival Canada's Cirque du Soleil.

4 Sanlitun
MAP H2 ■ Subway: Tuanjiehu

Beijing's main shopping, dining, and drinking district is centered around Taikoo Li and Nali Patio on Sanlitun Bei Lu, and around the Workers' Stadium on Gongren Tiyuchang Bei Lu. It has a high concentration of international restaurants (see p93) and lots of boutique shopping (see p92). Streets around here, although modern, are tree-lined and, with plenty of cafés for refreshment stops, it is a very pleasant district to wander in.

Shop-lined street in Sanlitun

5 Southeast Corner Watchtower (Dong Bian Men)

MAP G5 ■ South of Jianguo Men Nei Dajie ■ 8512 1554 ■ Subway: Jianguo Men ■ Open 8am–4:30pm daily ■ Adm

Just south of the Second Ring Road, a chunk of the old city wall survives, including the 15th-century Dong Bian Men watchtower. Visitors can climb onto the battlements, walk along the wall and see the graffiti carved by soldiers during the Boxer Rebellion (see p38).

Southeast Corner Watchtower

6 Chaoyang Park

1 Chaoyang Gongyuan Nanlu ■ Open 6am–9pm daily

Escape the traffic and noise of central Beijing in this oasis of greenery. Located next to the Central Business District, Beijing's biggest park was constructed in 1984 and has some-thing for everyone. There are extensive walking paths, jogging trails, bike pathways (bike-hire is available), and sports facilities, including an outdoor table tennis complex. An amusement park with fairground rides, boating lakes, and an artificial beach for kids keep families entertained.

7 Ghost Street

MAP F2 ■ Subway: Beixingqiao

Gui Jie, or Ghost Street, is a 1-mile (2-km) stretch of Dong Zhi Men Nei Dajie that come nightfall is jammed with customers frequenting its 100

ALTARED CITY

Ri Tan Park's Altar of the Sun is one of eight such cosmologically aligned altars in Beijing, along with the Altar of Heaven (Tian Tan; see pp16–17), the Altar of Agriculture (Xiannong Tan; now part of the Ancient Architecture Museum; see p77), the Altar of the Moon in the west of the city, the Altar of Earth (Di Tan, see p83), the Altar of the Country in Zhong Shan Park, the Altar of the Silkworm in Bei Hai Park, and the lost Altar of the Gods of Heaven.

---

or so restaurants, many of which remain open 24 hours. The air smells like Sichuan peppercorn and chilies amid a lively, party-like atmosphere. Sichuan and Hunan food is the big draw here, in particular spicy platters of crayfish and fiery hot pots.

8 Workers' Stadium

MAP G2 ■ Gongren Tiyuchang Bei Lu ■ 6522 5665 ■ Subway: Dong Si Shi Tiao

Originally built in 1959 as one of Mao's "Ten Great Buildings" to celebrate the tenth anniversary of the People's Republic of China, the Workers' Stadium was demolished and rebuilt in 2020 for a World Cup bid. It is home to Beijing's premier soccer club, Beijing Guo'an, and is the city's main venues for large-scale rock and pop concerts. Many of Beijing's glitzy nightclubs are adjacent to or very near the stadium.

9 Dong Yue Miao
MAP G3 ■ 141 Chaoyang
Men Wai Dajie ■ 6551 0151
■ Subway: Dongdaqiao ■ Open
8:30am–4:30pm Tue–Sun ■ Adm
This colorful, active temple dating
to the early 14th century is tended
by Daoist monks. The main courtyard
leads into the Hall of Tai Shan, with
statues of gods and their attendants.

Statues in the Dong Yue Miao temple

10 Ri Tan Park
MAP G4 ■ Guanghua Lu ■ 8561
6301 ■ Subway: Jianguo Men ■ Open
6am–10pm daily (Nov–Mar: to 9pm)
One of the city's oldest parks, Ri Tan
was laid out around a sacrificial altar
in the 16th century. The round altar
remains, ringed by a wall, but this is
very much a living park, filled daily
with people walking and exercising.
The park is well maintained and is
surrounded by restaurants and cafés.

Red lanterns hanging in Ri Tan Park

**A WALK FROM RI TAN PARK
TO SANLITUN**

▶ **MORNING**

Start the day at the **Southeast
Corner Watchtower**, for an
aerial view from one of Beijing's
last remaining city walls. Walk
to the **Ancient Observatory** (see
p89) to see ancient brass instruments (and another rooftop view).
Keep heading north, but take a
break in **Ri Tan Park**, one of the
city's more picturesque green
spots. The park is home to a
lake and the ruins of a sacrificial
altar, but it is better known for
the countless locals who come to
exercise, fly kites, do morning tai
chi, or to simply enjoy the view.

AFTERNOON

Head out of the park via the
eastern exit and grab lunch at
one of **Ri Tan Lu's** many cafés
before continuing north to the
vibrant **Dong Yue Miao** temple.
Stroll past the redeveloped
Workers' Stadium, then keep
heading north into **Sanlitun**
(see p89) for an afternoon of
shopping at Taikoo Li, an open-
air shopping mall with over
200 retail outlets. Check out
the numerous designer boutiques (see p92), and pick up
some chic, handmade ceramics
at **Spin** (see p92). For cheap
eats, try the **Taco Bar** (see p93),
or go to **Jing Yaa Tang** (see p93)
for something more upmarket.
Enjoy a nightcap at **La Social**
(see p58), a lively South American
bar, which serves great cocktails.

See map on p88 ←

Shops, Markets, and Malls

① Tailor Shops in Sanlitun
MAP H2 ▪ Xindong Lu (off Gongtibeilu) and Sanlitun Xijie

The streets to the west of Taikoo Li have several custom tailors who can accommodate your schedule.

Silk Street Market artist and vendor

② Silk Street Market
MAP G4 ▪ 8 Xiushui Dongjie, Jianwai Dajie ▪ 5169 9003

This five-story market is the place to get silk goods, such as ties, tablecloths, traditional clothes and dressing gowns. It is also filled with counterfeit designer goods *(see p61)*.

③ China World Shopping Mall
MAP H4 ▪ 1 Jianguo Men Wai Dajie ▪ 6505 2288

The Silk Market sells the counterfeits, but this elegant shopping mall is where you come for the originals.

④ Shin Kong Place (SKP)
87 Jianguo Lu ▪ 8078 8888

A Taiwanese chain, Shin Kong is a temple for luxury shopping and gourmet dining. It also marked the debut appearance of many elite brands in mainland China.

⑤ Sanlitun SOHO
MAP H2 ▪ South side of Gongren Tiyuchang Bei Lu ▪ 5878 8888

Characterized by some colorful funnel-shaped buildings, Sanlitun SOHO is a vast complex of shopping malls, offices, hotels, and private apartments. Numerous brand stores, banks, restaurants, and cafés occupy the first floor.

⑥ The Place
MAP H4 ▪ 9 Guanghua Lu

This open-air shopping mall nestled beneath an enormous upturned LED TV screen contains many international high-street fashion stores.

⑦ Parkview Green
MAP H4 ▪ 9 Dongdaqiao Lu ▪ 5690 7000

Chic, eco-friendly mall with a range of fashion wear and accessories – from fashionable traditional Chinese women's wear by Amelie Wang to watches and jewelry by Van Cleef & Arpels, plus displays of contemporary art and Salvador Dalí sculptures.

⑧ Spin
6 Dingfu Zhuang Xili, Chaoyang District ▪ 6437 8649

These stylish ceramics are more affordable here than in Spin's other bases in Shanghai and New York. Check out the "Seven Fortune" pots.

⑨ Taikoo Li Sanlitun
MAP H2 ▪ 6 Gongren Tiyuchang Bei Lu (corner Sanlitun Bei Lu) ▪ 6417 6110

The upscale Village has many brand stores including Apple and Adidas, plus a range of restaurants and bars.

⑩ Jenny Lou's
MAP G3 ▪ 6 Sanlitun Bei Xiang ▪ 6461 6928

Expat heaven, with Dutch cheese, German bread, and French wines.

Restaurants

PRICE CATEGORIES
For the equivalent of a meal for two made up of a range of dishes, served with two glasses of wine, and including service.
....
¥ under ¥250   ¥¥ ¥250–¥500
¥¥¥ over ¥500

1 Jing Yaa Tang
MAP H2 ■ 1/F The Opposite House Hotel, 11 Sanlitun Bei Lu ■ 6410 5230 ■ ¥¥¥

An elegant restaurant, Jin Yaa Tang specializes in mouth-watering roast duck and regional Chinese dishes such as Kung Pao chicken and dim sum.

2 Taco Bar
MAP H2 ■ Unit 10, Electrical Research Institute, Gongti Bei Lu ■ 6501 6026 ■ Closed Mon & lunch Tue–Fri ■ ¥

The fish tacos here are addictive. Add a pitcher of margarita, and you'll never want to leave.

Comfort food at Taco Bar

3 Mosto
MAP H2 ■ Nali Patio, 81 Sanlitun Bei Lu ■ 5208 6030 ■ ¥¥

A stylish restaurant (see p56) featuring Mediterranean cuisine. Try their delicious risotto and the superb cocktails served after dark.

4 Hatsune
MAP H4 ■ 2nd floor, Heqiao Building C, 8a Guanghua Dong Lu ■ 6415 3939 ■ ¥¥

A class act: this stylish Japanese restaurant specializes in California-style sushi rolls with creative fillings.

5 Country Kitchen
MAP H3 ■ Rosewood Beijing, Jingguang Centre, 1 Chaoyangmen Dajie ■ 6597 8888 ■ ¥¥¥

The chefs here masterfully recreate traditional Chinese recipes and classics with a twist in an open kitchen. Be sure to try the hand-pulled noodle dishes (see p57).

6 Bottega
MAP H2 ■ 18 Sanlitun Lu ■ 6416 1752 ■ ¥¥

This popular pizzeria offers pizzas and calzones with charcoal crusts made with imported ingredients.

7 Migas Mercado
MAP H4 ■ 7th Floor, China World Mall, 1 Jianguomenwai Dajie ■ 6500 7579 ■ ¥¥¥

With views of the CCTV Tower, Migas Mercado serves Spanish sharing plates such as salted cod and steamed eggplant, and oxtail in red wine. DJs spin on weekends.

8 In & Out
MAP H2 ■ 1 Sanlitun Beixiaojie ■ 8454 0086 ■ ¥¥

Try delightful Yunnan dishes with a contemporary twist here.

9 Cai Yi Xuan
MAP H1 ■ Four Seasons Beijing, 48 Liang Ma Qiao Lu ■ 5695 8520 ■ ¥¥¥

Enjoy Beijing's best dim sum, along with top Cantonese fare (see p57).

10 Taste of Dadong
MAP H4 ■ Parkview Green, 9 Dongdaqiao Lu ■ 8563 0016 ■ ¥¥

This casual restaurant from one of Beijing's most famous chefs, Dong Zhenxiang, is outstanding value.

See map on p88

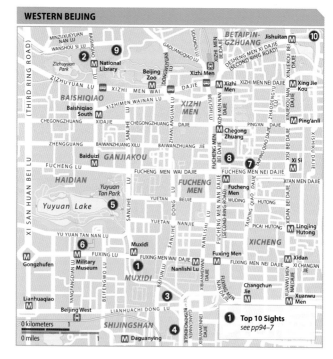 **Western Beijing**

Xicheng, meaning "West City," is the central district west of the Forbidden City and the lakes. Here, surrounding the White Dagoba Temple, are some of Beijing's most tourist-free *hutongs*. Western Beijing is best experienced as a series of half-day expeditions: a visit to the Capital Museum with a look at the White Cloud Temple afterward, or a boat ride in Yuyuan Tan Park, followed by a visit to the Military Museum. Expect to make liberal use of taxis and the subway.

Gilded bronze statue at the Capital Museum

1 Capital Museum
MAP B4 ▪ 16 Fuxing Men Wai Dajie, Xicheng ▪ 6337 0491 ▪ Subway: Muxidi ▪ Open 9am–5pm Tue–Sun ▪ en.capitalmuseum.org.cn

The Capital Museum celebrates China's civilization in general and Beijing's history in particular. The five-story building is easily recognizable thanks to its huge bronze cylinder. Exhibits include porcelain art, calligraphy, Buddha statues, furniture, and crafts. Reserve online.

WESTERN BEIJING

1 Top 10 Sights
see pp94–7

Immense reading room in the National Library of China

② National Library of China

MAP A1 ▪ 33 Zhongguancun Nandajie ▪ 8854 5426 ▪ Subway: National Library ▪ Open 9am–9pm Mon–Fri, 9am–5pm Sat & Sun (except pub hols) ▪ www.nlc.gov.cn

One of the five biggest libraries in the world, the National Library of China features a collection of approximately 12 million books. The building's floating roof houses the Digital Library. Most books are reference only, but visitors can request a reader's pass.

③ White Cloud Temple

MAP B4 ▪ 6 Baiyun Guan Jie, off Lianhuachi Dong Lu ▪ 6346 3531 ▪ Subway: Nanlishi Lu ▪ Open 8:30am–4:30pm daily (Oct 8–Apr: to 4pm) ▪ Adm

The first temple on this site was founded in AD 739 and burnt down in 1166. Since that time, it has been repeatedly destroyed and rebuilt. It even survived being used as a factory during the Cultural Revolution. The shrines, pavilions, and courtyards that make up the compound today date mainly from the Ming and Qing dynasties. Monks here are followers of Daoism and sport distinctive top-knots. Each Chinese New Year this is the venue for one of the city's most popular temple fairs, with performers, artisans, and traders.

④ Temple of Heavenly Tranquility (Tianning Si)

MAP B5 ▪ Guang'an Men Nanbinhe Lu ▪ Subway: Daguanying, then taxi

This temple, first built in the 5th century AD, is one of the city's oldest. The striking octagonal pagoda was added in the early 12th century and is original, making it possibly the oldest structure in Beijing. The bottom of the pagoda is decorated with carved arch patterns, symbolizing Sumeru, the mountain of the gods. Above are 13 levels of eaves.

Temple of Heavenly Tranquility

Brightly colored flower beds in full bloom at Yuyuan Tan Park

5 Yuyuan Tan Park
MAP A3 ▪ Xisanhuan Lu
▪ Subway: Military Museum ▪ Open
Dec–Mar: 6:30am–7pm daily; Apr,
May & Sep–Nov: 6am–8:30pm; Jun–
Aug: 6am–9:30pm ▪ Adm

Lovely Jade Lake Park is at its
most beautiful during cherry-
blossom season. Rent a boat
and traverse the massive
lakes, go for a swim, or
grab a snack from the
food stalls and have a
picnic – unusually for
Beijing – on the grass.

6 Military Museum of the Chinese People's Revolution
MAP A4 ▪ 9 Fuxing Lu
▪ 6686 6244 ▪ Subway:
Military Museum
▪ Open 8am–5pm
daily (passport
required for entry)

Vast halls of hardware
from the Cold War-era, including
lots of silvery fighter planes and
tanks, fill the first floor of this
interesting military museum. The
side halls have exhibitions on historic
conflicts, including the Opium Wars
and Boxer Rebellion (see p38). What
isn't mentioned is that the museum
is close to the Muxidi intersection,
scene of a massacre of civilians
by the Chinese army during the
democracy protests of 1989.

7 Miaoying Temple White Dagoba (Baita Si)
MAP C3 ▪ 171 Fucheng Men Nei
Dajie ▪ 6616 6099 ▪ Subway:
Fucheng Men ▪ Open 9am–4:30pm
daily ▪ Adm

Celebrated for its tall, Tibetan-style
white *dagoba* (stupa), this temple
dates to 1271, when Beijing
was under Mongol
rule. The view of it
looming over *hutong*
rooftops is one of the
most striking in Beijing.

8 Lu Xun Museum
MAP C3 ▪ 19 Gong
Men Kou Er Tiao, off Fucheng
Men Nei Dajie ▪ 6616 4080
▪ Subway: Fucheng Men
▪ Open 9am–4pm Tue–Sun

Lu Xun is regarded as
the father of modern
Chinese literature,
responsible for

**Statue in Miaoying
Temple White Dagoba**

BUDDHISM IN CHINA

Buddhism started in India and probably
came to China along the Silk Road. The
earliest sign of the religion is linked to
the founding of the White Horse Temple
near the old capital of Luoyang in
AD 68. Buddhism surged in popularity
during periods of instability, when
Confucianism's veneration for authority
did not sit well with the populace. It was
eventually adopted by China's rulers.

such ground-breaking works as "Diary of a Madman" and "The True Story of Ah Q". This museum complex contains the house in which he lived from 1924 to 1926. Among the artifacts relating to his life are more than 10,000 letters, journals, photographs, and other personal objects.

⑨ Temple of the Five Pagodas

MAP B1 ■ 24 Wuta Si Cun ■ 6217 3836 ■ Subway: National Museum or Xizhi Men ■ Open 8:30am–5pm Tue–Sun ■ Adm

This temple displays obvious Indian influences. Built in the early 15th century, it honors the Indian monk who came to China and presented the emperor with five golden Buddhas. The pagodas sport elaborate carvings of curvaceous females, as well as the customary Buddhas. Also here is the Beijing Art Museum of Stone Carvings, with historic stelae and statues.

Deshengmen Arrow Tower

⑩ Deshengmen Arrow Tower

MAP D1 ■ 19 Xinjiekouwai Dajie ■ Open 9am–4pm Tue–Sun ■ Adm

A restored chunk of Beijing's city wall, this impressive arrow tower would have stood in front of one of Beijing's nine former city gates. The tower itself holds exhibits on old weapons. Rooms below house the Beijing Ancient Coins Museum, which tells the history of money in China from ancient "shell" coins to the Republic of China paper bills.

WAR AND PEACE

▶ **MORNING**

Even if you're no big fan of mechanized heavy armor, the **Military Museum of the Chinese People's Revolution** is worth a visit. Exhibits begin with the technology that made China one of the world's first military superpowers, including the "Flying Dragon," an early form of missile launcher. Keep an eye out for the gifts that have been bestowed on China's army chiefs and leaders, such as a pistol presented to Chairman Mao by Fidel Castro. Mao's limousine is sometimes on display, and one area is devoted to statues and assorted representations of the Communist Party's great and good. It all makes for a fascinating insight into the mentality of late 20th-century China.

AFTERNOON

Leaving the museum, walk west along Fuxing Lu and take the first right. You will see the **Millennium Monument** and, behind it, **Yuyuan Tan Park**, a relaxing place for a stroll. Pick up a snack from one of the vendors here and have a picnic, or try the borscht and vodka at the venerable **Moscow Restaurant** *(135 Xizhimenwai Dajie)*, beside the Millennium Monument before continuing on Fuxing Men Wai Dajie toward Muxidi and the **Capital Museum** *(see p94)*. Audio self-guided tours in Chinese and English are available at the entrance. Don't miss the Timeline of Beijing exhibition in Hall C and the Qianlong emperor's vast stelae on display outside the museum's entrance.

See map on p94 ←

🔟 Greater Beijing

Beijing is vast. Although you could spend all your time without ever straying too far from the area around Tian'an Men Square, you would be missing out on a lot. Sights in the northwest of the city include the unmissable Summer Palace, the intoxicating hillside Xiang Shan Park and the haunting ruins of the Yuanming Yuan, or Old Summer Palace. For fans of contemporary urban culture, the 798 Art District in Beijing's northeast is a must, and you can drop in on the markets and bars around Sanlitun on the way back into town.

The lakeside Summer Palace

1 Summer Palace

The grounds of what was once the royal retreat of emperors make up one of China's most famous and largest classical gardens. The garden is arranged as a microcosm of nature, with hills and water complemented by bridges, temples, and walkways. It manages to be both fanciful and harmonious at the same time.

GREATER BEIJING

Baiwangshan Forest Park
Qing River
Lincuiqiao
Forest South
Beijing Botanical Gardens ⑥
Anheqiao North Ⓜ
S 50 BEI WU HUAN
G JING ZANG GAO SU
National Olympic Stadium ⑩
Yuanming Yuan (Old Summer Palace) ②
Summer Palace ① Xiyuan Ⓜ
③ Xiang Shan Park
Kunming Lake
HAIDIANZHEN
DONGSHENGXIANG
BEI SI HUAN XI LU
National Aquatics Center ⑧
Forest Park
ZHONGGUANCUN
Xitucheng Ⓜ
Science and Technology Museum ⑨
Badachu Park
Beijing Xijiao Airport ✈
Haidian Huangzhuang Ⓜ
④ Great Bell Temple (Dazhong Temple)
Weigongcun Ⓜ
Yonghe Lama Te
HAIDIAN
SIJIQINGZHEN
Beijing North Railway Station 🚆
Jishuitan
Chedaogou Ⓜ

0 kilometers   3
0 miles   3

Ruins at Yuanming Yuan (Old Summer Palace)

2 Yuanming Yuan (Old Summer Palace)

28 Qinghua Xi Lu ▪ 6262 8501
▪ Subway: Yuanming Yuan Park
▪ Open 7am–7pm daily (Sep & Oct: to 6:30pm; Nov–Mar: to 5:30pm) ▪ Adm
▪ www.yuanmingyuanpark.cn

The palace's name can be translated as "Garden of Perfect Brightness." It was the largest and most elaborate of all the summer palaces of the Qing era. It once contained private imperial residences, pleasure pavilions, a vast imperial ancestral shrine, Buddhist temples, and canals and lakes. The Qianlong emperor even added a group of European-style palaces designed by Jesuit missionary-artists serving in the Qing court. Today, only graceful ruins remain, after the ravaging effects of the Second Opium War (1856–60), when British and French troops burned down the whole site.

3 Xiang Shan Park

Wofosi Lu ▪ 6259 1264
▪ Subway: Fragrant Hills
▪ Open 6am–6:30pm daily (Jul & Aug: to 7pm; mid-Nov–Mar: to 6pm) ▪ Adm
▪ www.xiangshanpark.com

The hillside Xiang Shan parkland, also known as Fragrant Hills Park, is 2 miles (3 km) west of the Summer Palace. It offers fine views from Incense Burner Peak, which is accessible by a chairlift (for a fee). Close to the park's main gate is the Azure Clouds Temple (Biyun Si), guarded by the menacing deities Heng and Ha in the Mountain Gate Hall. A series of halls leads to the Sun Yat Sen Memorial Hall, where the revolutionary leader's coffin was stored in 1925, before being taken to his final resting place in Nanjing.

4 Great Bell Temple (Dazhong Temple)

MAP B1 ▪ 31A Beisanhuan Xi Lu
▪ 6255 0819 ▪ Subway: Dazhongsi
▪ Open 9am–4:30pm daily ▪ Adm

This 18th-century temple has been taken over by a fascinating and modern museum all about bells, both instrumental and religious. The showpiece attraction is the massive bell – one of the world's largest – housed in the rear tower. The bell was cast between 1403 and 1424, and has Buddhist *sutras* in Chinese and Sanskrit on its surface.

Top 10 Sights
see pp98–101

Ornate bell at the Great Bell Temple

Graffiti art on a wall in the 798 Art District

5 798 Art District

Although it's called the 798 Art District (see pp30–31), known locally as Da Shan Zi, Factory number 798 is only one of the several former industrial units taken over by artists and galleries. The complex features many of Beijing's best galleries, including UCCA and M Woods Art Museum.

Lily pond, Beijing Botanical Gardens

6 Beijing Botanical Gardens

6259 1283 ▪ Subway: Botanical Garden ▪ Open 7am–5pm daily ▪ Adm ▪ www.beijingbg.com

About a mile (2 km) northeast of Xiang Shan Park lie these pretty gardens, containing some 3,000 plant species and pleasant walks. The garden's Sleeping Buddha Temple (Wofo Si) is renowned for its magnificent 15-ft (5-m) bronze statue of a reclining Buddha. China's last emperor, Pu Yi (see p13), worked here in his later years as a gardener.

7 China National Film Museum

9 Nanying Road, Caochangdi Village, Chaoyang ▪ 8435 5959 ▪ Bus: 418 from Dong Zhi Men ▪ Open 9am–4:30pm Tue–Sun (last adm 3:30pm) ▪ www.cnfm.org.cn

Reportedly the world's largest, this film museum is housed in a glass-and-steel structure and features 20 exhibition halls, an IMAX theater, a digital projection theater, and several 35mm theaters. Over 100 years of Chinese cinema are represented by 1,500 films and 4,300 stills from the works of 450 film-makers.

CHINA'S PEOPLES

China's 1.41 billion population includes about 55 different ethnic minorities, each with their own languages and, in many cases, distinctive customs. Though rich in culture, and varied, together these ethnic minorities make up only eight percent of the population, with the main group, known as Han Chinese, accounting for the rest.

⑧ National Aquatics Center (Water Cube)

This 2008 Olympic venue proves there is life after the Games – the Water Cube (see p44) became a water park, before it was re-purposed to host the 2022 Winter Games' curling events. In this collaboration between Chinese and Australian architects, China drew from the classical mythology tradition of a square earth and round heaven, symbolized here by the angled building and the circular stadium. The Australians designed the bubbles, representing soap lather's natural pattern.

Science and Technology Museum

⑨ Science and Technology Museum

MAP E1 ■ 1 Beisanhuan Zhong Lu ■ 6237 1177 ■ Subway: Olympic Park ■ Open 9:30am–5pm Tue–Sat ■ Adm ■ www.cstm.org.cn

Exhibits begin with ancient science, highlighting China's "technological pre-eminence in history." The technology comes up to date with Chinese space capsules, robots, and an Astro-vision Theater incorporating state-of-the-art cinematography.

⑩ National Olympic Stadium (Bird's Nest)

Inspired by Chinese ceramics, the design of interlocking steel beams was initially supporting a retractable roof. This was later removed, but what remains is still a stunning structure. Between staging both winter and summer Olympics, the Bird's Nest (see p44) has hosted everything from soccer matches to pop concerts.

GREEN BEIJING

▶ **MORNING**

Be at the East Gate (Dong Men) of the **Summer Palace** (see p28–9) for 8:30am to beat both the heat (if you are visiting in summer) as well as the crowds. Make your way along the north shore of Kunming Lake via the Long Corridor (see p28) and ascend **Longevity Hill** (see p29). Descend again to the Marble Boat and take a pleasure cruiser across the lake to **South Lake Island**. Cross back to the mainland via the supremely elegant **Seventeen-Arch Bridge** (see p29); exit via the South Gate and take the Xijiao light rail line to **Xiang Shan Park** (see p99), otherwise known as Fragrant Hills Park. Before you enter, grab a bite to eat at one of the several cafés and restaurants outside the East Gate.

AFTERNOON

From the park's East Gate, turn right for the **Temple of Brilliance**, built in 1780 and ransacked by Western troops in 1860 and 1900. Close by is the **Liuli Pagoda**, with bells hanging from its eaves that chime in the breeze. Continue north to pass between two small round lakes linked by a small hump-backed bridge – the whole known as the **Spectacles Lakes**. Beyond is a chairlift that takes you up to the top of the "Fragrant Hill." Zigzag back down past many more pavilions to arrive at the **Fragrant Hills Hotel**, designed by Chinese-American architect I. M. Pei, best known for his glass pyramid at the Louvre in Paris and the Suzhou Museum near Shanghai.

See map on pp98–9 ←

🔟 Farther Afield

Beijing has more than enough sights to keep the average visitor busy. However, after traveling all this way, it would be a shame not to grasp the opportunity to get out of the city. Of course, the Great Wall of China is high on the list for any visitor, but beyond the bustle of Beijing there are also ancient temples nestled on green hillsides and the vast necropolis of the Ming emperors. To the southwest is the 300-year-old stone Marco Polo Bridge and neighboring Wanping, a rare surviving example of a walled city dating to the 17th century. Both are an easy suburban bus ride from Beijing.

Imposing statuary at the Ming Tombs

FARTHER AFIELD

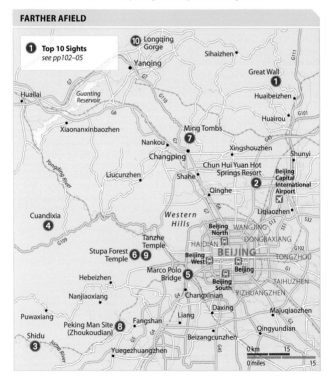

A stretch of the Great Wall of China surrounded by green hills

1 Great Wall

When in China, a visit to the Great Wall is a must. The closest major section to Beijing is at Badaling, and you can get there and back in half a day. However, if you suspect that your appreciation of this matchless monument would be improved by the absence of coach-loads of fellow tourists, then you might want to consider traveling that little bit farther to the sites at Mutianyu, Gubeikou, and Jinshanling *(see pp34–5)*. This area tends to be fiercely hot in the summer, and bitterly cold in the winter. Go prepared with sunscreen and lots of water on warmer days, and with warm clothing layers on colder ones.

2 Chun Hui Yuan Hot Springs Resort

20 miles (33 km) N of Beijing ■ 6945 4433 ■ Bus 942 from Dong Zhi Men to Yu Zhuang, from the stop, turn left and walk just over 1 mile (2 km) to the resort, or take a taxi from Beijing ■ www.chunhuiyuan.cn

After a day of hiking or rock climbing, unwind at the Chun Hui Yuan Hot Springs Resort. Sink into a hot tub, swim in the pool, try a sauna, or book a spa treatment. Everything here is geared toward total rejuvenation.

3 Shidu

62 miles (100 km) SW of Beijing ■ 6134 9009 ■ Bus 917 from Tianqiao station

With its stunning natural scenery, Shidu offers a fabulous escape from the commotion of urban Beijing. In the olden days, travelers had to cross the Juma River ten times to journey through Shidu and nearby Zhangfang village. The name Shidu means "Ten Crossings." Pleasant walking trails wind along the riverbank between impressive gorges and limestone formations. Also located here are four vertigo-inducing glass bridges.

Boating at the gorge in Shidu

The mountainside village of Cuandixia

④ Cuandixia
Near Zhaitang town, 56 miles (90 km) W of Beijing ▪ 6981 9333 ▪ Subway: Pingguo Yuan (1 hr), then taxi, or bus 892 (3 daily, last bus back at 3:35pm) ▪ Adm

On a steep mountainside, Cuandixia is a picturesque hamlet of courtyard houses (siheyuan), most dating from the Ming and Qing dynasties. A ticket allows access to the entire village, which can be explored in a few hours. The population consists of about 29 families. Those wanting an experience of rural hospitality can arrange accommodations with a local family.

⑤ Marco Polo Bridge
10 miles (16 km) SW of Beijing ▪ 8389 2521 ▪ Subway: Dawayao, then taxi or bus 339 ▪ Open 7am–8pm daily (Nov–Apr: to 6pm)

Straddling the Yongding River near the reconstructed Wanping fortress, this marble bridge, also known as Lugou Bridge, was first built during the Jin dynasty in 1189 but was destroyed by a flood. The current structure dates to 1698, and acquires its name from Marco Polo's description of it in his treatise *The Travels*. The balustrades along the length of the bridge are decorated with over 400 stone lions, each one different from the rest. On July 7, 1937, the Japanese Imperial Army and Nationalist Chinese soldiers exchanged fire here, leading to war and the Japanese occupation of Beijing.

⑥ Stupa Forest Temple (Talin Si)
28 miles (45 km) W of Beijing ▪ 6086 2505 ▪ Subway: Pingguo Yuan (1 hr), then bus 931 ▪ Open 8am–5pm daily ▪ Adm

Near the parking lot for the Tanzhe Temple is this even more fascinating temple, notable for its collection of brick stupas hidden among the foliage. Every stupa was built in memory of a renowned monk. The towering edifices were built in a variety of designs, and the earliest dates from the Jin dynasty (1115–1234).

⑦ Ming Tombs
The Ming Tombs (see pp32–3) are the resting place for 13 of the 16 Ming emperors. These are Confucian shrines and follow a standard layout of a series of courtyards and a main hall, with a "soul tower" and burial mound beyond. The tombs are not as colorful and elaborate as Buddhist and Daoist structures, and only three are open to the public, but the necropolis is a worthwhile stop-off as part of an excursion to the Great Wall.

Bronze statue at the Ming Tombs

Diorama at the Peking Man Site

⑧ Peking Man Site (Zhoukoudian)

30 miles (48 km) SW of Beijing ▪ 6930 1278 ▪ Bus 917 or 836 from Beijing's Tianqiao station to Fangshan, then taxi or bus 38 ▪ Open 8:30am–4:30pm daily ▪ Adm

In the 1920s, archeologists removed from a cave at Zhoukoudian some 40-odd fossilized bones and primitive implements, which they identified as the prehistoric remains of Peking Man. It was thought that this exciting discovery provided the much sought-after link between Neanderthals and modern humans. Designated a UNESCO World Heritage Site, the area is geared toward specialists,

---

MARCO POLO

Whether Venetian trader and explorer Marco Polo (1254–1324) ever visited China is much disputed. The book he dictated to a ghost writer, who embroidered it substantially, describes aspects of Far Eastern life in much detail, including paper money, the Grand Canal, the structure of a Mongol army, tigers, and the bridge that now bears his name. *The Travels of Marco Polo*, however, may be based on earlier journeys by his father and uncles, and stories from Arab Silk Road merchants.

---

although the small museum has an interesting collection of tools and bone fragments. Peking Man himself is not here – his remains mysteriously disappeared during World War II.

⑨ Tanzhe Temple

28 miles (45 km) W of Beijing ▪ 6086 2505 ▪ Subway: Pingguo Yuan (1 hr), then bus 931 ▪ Open 8am–5pm daily ▪ Adm

This enormous temple dates back to the 3rd century AD, when it was known as Jiafu Si. It was later renamed for the adjacent mountain, Tanzhe Shan. It has a splendid mountainside setting, and its halls rise up the steep incline. The temple is especially famous for its odd-shaped, ancient trees. Restaurants here may be over-priced, so bring your own lunch.

Colorful model of Longqing Gorge

⑩ Longqing Gorge

25 miles (40 km) NW of Beijing ▪ Express bus 919 (5:45am–7pm) from Deshengmen station; get off at Yanqing Dongguan, then take bus Y15 or a taxi to Longqingxia ▪ Open 7:30am–4:30pm daily (during Ice Lantern Festival, Jan & Feb: 9am–10pm daily) ▪ Adm

About 25 miles (40 km) away from the bustle of Beijing, this area has lush landscapes. Adventure seekers can go bungee-jumping and zip-lining. Those wanting a more relaxing break can visit the Diamond Temple or go up to the top of the dam using the 846-ft- (258-m-) long Dragon Escalator.

See map on p102

Streetsmart

Red lanterns hanging for the New
Year's celebrations at Di Tan Park

Getting Around

Arriving by Air

Beijing has two international airports. **Beijing Capital Airport** is closer to the city center and has better public transport connections than the newer **Beijing Daxing Airport**. Both airports have direct links to countless national and international destinations with China's flagship carrier, **Air China**, as well as international lines **China Airlines**, **China Eastern**, and **China Southern**, plus numerous local carriers. It's also worth checking flights that arrive at neighboring Tianjin and taking the 30- to 40-minute bullet train, which runs every 10 to 15 minutes to Beijing, and costs ¥54.5.

A taxi from Capital Airport to central Beijing should cost ¥100–150, including the ¥5 toll, depending on your location and traffic. A taxi from Daxing Airport costs around Y200–Y250. Make sure your driver uses the meter, and have your hotel's name and phone number written down in Chinese. It is best to avoid the illegal drivers who approach you at the airport.

Both airports have dedicated shuttle train services into Beijing. A cheaper option from Beijing Capital, at ¥25, is the **Beijing Airport Express**, a subway line that takes 20 minutes to get to Dong Zhi Men. The **Daxing Airport Express** connects the airport with Beijing's subway network at Caoqiao (Line 10), from where it's another 50 minutes into the center of town.

Arriving by Sea

Beijing is a landlocked city, but ferries from Taiwan, South Korea, and Japan disembark at **Tianjin Port (Tianjin Xingang)**, from where you can take the subway, a bus or a taxi (around ¥25) to Tanggu Railway Station for the bullet train.

Arriving by Train

China's extensive train network is an excellent way to travel. Most trains these days are high-speed bullet trains, but the older trains can be fun for slow travel. The hub of China's travel industry, Beijing offers direct international routes to Ulaanbaatar, Moscow, Hanoi, and Pyongyang from Beijing Railway Station (subway line 2), South Railway Station (lines 4 and 14), and West Railway Station (lines 7 and 9). North Railway Station (also called Xizhimen Station, lines 2, 4 and 13) is for domestic travel. The large Fengtai Railway Station (lines 10 and 16) in the south of the city offers high-speed and regular train services to all parts of China.

Trains come in an alphabet of classes, from G, the highest-level speed train, with business class and soft sleepers, to K, with hard and soft seats, hard and soft sleepers, and deluxe soft sleepers. The hard sleeper is adequate, but avoid the hard seats. Numbered trains are the slowest and have seats only. Stations are signposted in Chinese and English, but it's best to arrive at any station one to two hours early to navigate the crowds. Avoid travel during holiday "golden" weeks, May 1 and October 1.

Arriving by Bus

There are several long-distance bus stations scattered around Beijing. However, with the availability of cheap, high-speed rail travel all over the country, there's little need for travellers to use intercity buses, which are far slower.

Public Transport

Subway trains and buses are the primary modes of public transport in Beijing. There is no single transport authority. A rechargeable Yikatong card is the best way to pay for public transport. This can be bought at subway stations, bus stations, and some supermarkets for a ¥20 deposit, then topped up as needed. It can be used for the subway, buses, taxis, and "S" suburban trains to the Great Wall, and unused money can be refunded.

Subway

Beijing's subway network is the most efficient way of getting around and avoiding the city's frequently heavy traffic.

There are 22 subway lines, with more on the way. The fare varies with distance, but you can get almost anywhere for ¥6 to ¥10. Frequent trains operate from 5am to 11:30pm. Ticket machines, subway maps, signs and announcements are in Chinese and English. **Travel China Guide** has the latest subway maps.

Buses

For non-Chinese speakers, buses are harder to navigate than the subway, but show the Chinese name of your destination to a friendly passenger and they'll tell you when to alight. Use cash (fares range between ¥1 to ¥12 depending on distance) or your Yikatong card, which will get you a discount of up to 60 percent. The **Tour Beijing** and Travel China Guide websites have details of bus routes and prices.

Taxis

Taxis are pretty affordable but journey times can be long as the city is often plagued by heavy traffic, especially in morning and evening rush hours. Never take an unmetered taxi, and avoid parked cars outside tourist attractions; flag down a taxi in the street instead or go to one of the official taxi ranks, which are scattered all over the city. Black (illegal) cabs are regular cars marked with a horizontal red windshield light; these should be avoided as they are not reliable for price or safety.

In rush hour and when it is raining heavily it can be difficult to hail a taxi in the street but ride sharing apps such as DiDi Ride (China's equivalent to Uber), which has an English interface, can be booked more easily. DiDi Ride is incompatible with non-Chinese credit cards but you can pay the fare on the meter in cash.

Few taxi drivers speak English so for every taxi journey make sure you have the destination written down in Chinese to show to the driver.

Cycling

Cycling can be a good way to see Beijing, particularly the *hutongs* and historical areas. The city is very flat, making it ideal for getting around on two wheels but high pollution levels can be a deterrent. Some hostels and hotels offer bike rental.

Inexperienced cyclists should take care: e-bike riders and cyclists don't always stop at red lights, and they frequently drive and ride on the wrong side of the road. There are wide bike lanes everywhere, but cars sometimes use them as parking lots, which forces the riders into the streets. Watch out for cyclists and pedestrians who pull out or step out into the road suddenly without looking. It's best first to try cycling in the quieter *hutongs* to gauge your comfort level. Once you're out in the city traffic, being a proactive, defensive rider is the best course of action.

Walking

Beijing is vast and the sights are widespread so it is best explored in small sections if you're getting around on foot. Walking is one of the best ways to experience the old *hutong* neighborhoods.

DIRECTORY

ARRIVING BY AIR

Air China
🌐 airchina.com.cn

Beijing Airport Express
🌐 en.bcia.com.cn/traffic/express

Beijing Capital Airport
🌐 en.bcia.com.cn

Beijing Daxing Airport
🌐 bdia.com.cn

China Airlines
🌐 china-airlines.com

China Eastern
🌐 en.ceair.com

China Southern
🌐 csair.com/en/index.shtml

Daxing Airport Express
🌐 daxing-pkx-airport.com

ARRIVING BY SEA

Tianjin Port (Tianjin Xingang)
🌐 ptacn.com

ARRIVING BY BUS

Dongzhimen Station
📞 6467 1346

SUBWAY

China Travel Guide
🌐 travelchinaguide.com/cityguides/beijing/transportation

BUS

Tour Beijing
🌐 tour-beijing.com/public_bus

Practical Information

Passports and Visas

For the latest entry requirements, including visas, consult your nearest Chinese embassy or the **Chinese Visa Applications Service Center** website. A passport, valid for at least six months, and a visa are necessary to enter the People's Republic of China. Most foreign nationals don't require a visa for entering Hong Kong and Macau but will need one if traveling on to mainland China. Visas must be obtained from your home/resident country from either the Chinese Embassy or Consulate, or in their affiliate Visa Application Service Center. Tourists can get a single/multiple-entry, 30-day to 6-month tourist visa, although UK, US, Canadian, Argentinian, and Israeli citizens can get a 10-year multiple-entry visa if they have visited China previously. Apply as early as possible and allow at least one month for your visa to be processed. When completing the visa application, you are usually required to provide proof of a return ticket, an itinerary, and hotel bookings for your entire trip.

Government Advice

Now more than ever, it is important to consult both your and the Chinese government's advice before traveling. The **UK Foreign, Commonwealth & Development Office (FCDO)**, the **US Department of State**, the **Australian Department of Foreign Affairs and Trade**, and the **Government of the People's Republic of China** offer the latest information on security, health, and local regulations.

Customs Information

You can find information on the laws relating to goods and currency taken in or out of China on the **General Administration of Customs People's Republic of China** website. At politically sensitive times, books brought into China may be examined, and anti-China material will be confiscated.

Insurance

It is important to take out a comprehensive insurance policy covering theft, loss of belongings, medical care, cancellations, and delays, and to read the small print carefully. Private medical healthcare in China is very expensive, so it is especially important to have good medical cover.

Health

Healthcare in China centers on public and private hospitals and the quality of care in Beijing is good. Public hospitals are very affordable but staff are less likely to speak English. When visiting these, including **Peking Union Medical College Hospital**'s international department, you may need an interpreter.

Private international hospitals, such as **Beijing United Family Hospital**, **Raffles Medical**, and **Hong Kong International Medical Clinic, Beijing**, have English-speaking doctors but are much more expensive so it is important to have medical insurance. You will need to pay upfront for medical care and reclaim the cost from your insurance company later.

Pharmacies provide good advice on minor ailments and sell both Western and traditional Chinese medicines. The pharmacy at Beijing United Family Hospital is particularly good for buying over-the-counter medicine and getting advice in English.

Those concerned about pollution can download an app for hourly reports. Donning a 2.5PM mask and planning indoor activities on days when pollution is particularly high is advised. It is best to avoid drinking tap water, so to be safe drink bottled or filtered water at all times. Western digestive systems can struggle with the oil in Chinese food, so it's a good idea to bring anti-diarrhea medicine.

Ensure routine vaccinations, such as tetanus and polio, are up to date. It is also wise to get vaccinated against hepatitis A and B, and typhoid. Visitors traveling from countries where yellow fever is endemic must provide proof of vaccination against the disease. For information regarding

COVID-19 vaccination requirements, consult government advice.

Smoking, Alcohol, and Drugs

Alcohol is widely available in China; and the national drink is baijiu, a very strong spirit. The legal age is 18 for both drinking and purchasing alcohol. Smoking is banned in all enclosed public places, including on public transport. Possessing or testing positive for illegal substances carries severe penalties, including fines, deportation, imprisonment, and even a death sentence. Random testing has been known to take place, as have raids on nightclubs and bars.

ID

Carry your passport with you at all times. Police carry out random checks and failure to produce your ID can lead to a fine or detention. You will also need your passport for entry into many museums in Beijing, including the Forbidden City.

Personal Security

Beijing is a relatively safe city, and most visits are trouble-free but petty crime is not unusual. Use common sense: keep belongings close and be alert to your surroundings, especially in crowded places. Beware of scams in tourist areas: you may be invited to a bar or a teahouse and then be stuck with a massive bill. Spiking of drinks has been known, so do not leave drinks unattended and avoid accepting drinks from strangers. Women traveling alone or with female friends may be particularly at risk of this.

If you have anything stolen, report the crime within 24 hours to the nearest police station. If you need to make an insurance claim, get a copy of the crime report.

Contact your embassy if your passport is stolen, or in the event of a serious crime or accident.

Demonstrations should be avoided; Chinese authorities enforce public order strictly and you may face arrest, detention, and/or deportation. For emergency **police** call 110, in case of **fire** call 119, and for an **ambuance** call 120 (though it is best to take a taxi to the nearest hospital rather than wait for an ambulance).

Homosexuality has been legal in China since 1997, but there are no anti-discrimination laws and same-sex marriage has not been legalized. China remains a largely conservative society and overt displays of affection (regardless of sexual orientation) may garner raised eyebrows. Nevertheless, attitudes among young Beijingers are more embracing and there is a modest but growing LGBTQ+ scene centered in the Sanlitun area.

DIRECTORY

PASSPORTS AND VISAS

Chinese Visa Applications Service Center
w visaforchina.org

GOVERNMENT ADVICE

Australian Department of Foreign Affairs and Trade
w smartraveller.gov.au
w dfat.gov.au/travel

Government of the People's Republic of China
w english.www.gov.cn

UK Foreign, Commonwealth & Development Office (FCDO)
w gov.uk/foreign-travel-advice

US Department of State
w travel.state.gov

CUSTOMS INFORMATION

General Administration of Customs People's Republic of China
w english.customs.gov.cn

HEALTH

Beijing United Family Hospital
w beijing.ufh.com.cn

Hong Kong International Medical Clinic, Beijing
w hkclinic.com

Raffles Medical
w rafflesmedicalgroup.com/beijing

Peking Union Medical College Hospital
w pumch.cn

PERSONAL SECURITY

Ambulance
c 120

Fire
c 119

Police
c 110

Travelers with Specific Requirements

Since the 2022 Winter Olympic Games, Beijing has made some progress in meeting the needs of travelers with accessibility requirements. There are curb ramps and tactile guide paths in much of the city. However, only top attractions and some five-star hotels have ramps and accessible hand rails. Not all subways and buses have wheelchair access but there are an increasing number of wheelchair-friendly taxis. On the plus side, most Chinese people are very accommodating and resourceful, and do their best to make things as easy as possible.

Time Zone

Beijing is eight hours ahead of GMT, 13 hours ahead of New York, and two hours behind Sydney. The city does not use Daylight Saving Time.

Money

The national currency is the *yuan* (¥), also known as *renminbi* or *kuai* (slang). Most major credit cards are accepted in shopping malls and international hotels and restaurants. While it is still possible to make cash payments, China is fast becoming a cashless society. Most Chinese use mobile payment systems such as **WeChat Pay** and **Alipay** to pay for all goods and services, including street market and other small purchases. WeChat has partnered with major international credit cards, including Visa, Master-Card, and American Express, to allow foreign visitors to add their credit cards directly to their digital wallet on the WeChat app. The Alipay app functions as a prepaid credit card onto which foreign visitors can add funds from an international credit or debit card and then use it on a pay-as-you-go basis.

Tipping is not customary or expected and can be considered rude. However, in more expensive hotels and restaurants catering to Western tourists, room service and porters may be more accustomed to receiving small tips of 5–30 yuan or 10–15 per cent of the bill.

Electrical Appliances

Electrical current is 220 volts AC, so North Americans should use dual-voltage appliances or a converter. China uses two parallel flat pins, two parallel round pins, or two or three slanted flat pins – and some sockets accept all of these. Buying a universal adapter is advisable

Cell Phones and Wi-Fi

China operates on the GSM network so most cell phones brought overseas will work with a local SIM card. You can purchase a SIM card at the airport or at local shops. **China Unicom**, **China Telecom**, and **China Mobile** are the main network providers.

Free Wi-Fi is available at most restaurants, cafés, and hotels. You'll need a VPN to access Facebook, Google, and most Western sites unless you use your own phone's international roaming service. Two of the most popular VPN services are ExpressVPN and Astrill, but this situation is fluid, so check reviews and sign up for free trials before your trip. Apple maps can easily be accessed but Google maps only works with a VPN, or try the **Gaode** or **Baidu** Chinese map websites. WeChat offers free audio and video calls and messaging to local and international users.

Postal Services

Open 9am–5pm daily, **China Post** has several branches in Beijing, but *kuadi* (couriers) are usually faster. For next-day deliveries within the city, ask your hotel to arrange a *kuadi*.

Weather

Temperate weather makes both spring and autumn the ideal seasons to visit the city. During summer, temperatures range from 80° F (27° C) to a soaring 105° F (41° C), while winter can be anywhere from 26° F (-3° C) to 16° F (-9° C). Beijing generally has a dry climate, but summer sees frequent rain as well as some hailstorms, while winter tends to have the heaviest pollution.

Opening Hours

International restaurants are usually open from 10am to 10pm, but Chinese restaurants tend to close earlier at around 8:30pm, and in the afternoon from 2 to 5pm, except for the 24-hour venues on Gui Jie. Many convenience stores and street food stalls are open until at least 11pm. Other shops and supermarkets usually open from 9am to 8pm, and banks and pharmacies operate from 9am to 5pm. Museums and attractions are usually open from 9am to 4:30pm, but some have shorter winter hours, and nearly all are closed on Mondays.

The COVID-19 pandemic proved that situations can change suddenly. Always check before visiting attractions and hospitality venues for up-to-date hours and booking requirements.

Visitor Information

Beijing Tourism has useful information on its website. There are tourist offices in each airport terminal and around the city. A number of operators run tours.

Travel China Guide, **China Highlights**, and **Discover Beijing Tours** offer standard packages and day trips. Or try **Bespoke Travel Company**'s customized tours.

Local Customs

Despite widespread modernization, China remains a largely traditional society and retains a deep-seated and family-oriented conservatism. Confucian values promote respect for elders and those in positions of authority, and reinforce notions of conformity. Chinese people can be very direct, and will not blanch at asking personal questions. This is seen as taking an interest in a new acquaintance. The maintenance of pride and the avoidance of shame is very important and known as saving face. Loss of face *(mianzi)* creates discomfort and embarrassment for the Chinese, so try tackling difficult situations by being patient, firm, and polite, and avoid confrontation.

Language

The official language of China is Mandarin. It is a tonal language that uses pictographic characters rather than a set alphabet. Pinyin is a Romanization system of Mandarin that helps in the recognition of sounds and bands with diacritical marks to indicate tones. Many Beijingers speak basic English at tourist sights, but learning a few phrases of Mandarin will go a long way.

Taxes and Refunds

Foreign tourists who have stayed on the Chinese mainland for less than 183 consecutive days are entitled to a departure tax refund of 13 per cent, minus a 2 per cent service fee, under certain conditions. This applies to a minimum spend of ¥500 in the same tax-refund shop in Beijing on the same day. Take the tax refund form issued by the store to the Customs desk at your airport of departure to receive your refund.

DIRECTORY

MONEY

Alipay
w global.alipay.com

WeChat Pay
w pay.weixin.qq.com

CELL PHONES AND WI-FI

Baidu
w baidu.com

China Mobile
w chinamobiletd.com

China Telecom
w chinatelecomglobal.com

China Unicorn
w chinaunicorn.com

Gaode
w gaode.com

POSTAL SERVICES

China Post
w english.chinapost.com.cn

VISITOR INFORMATION

Beijing Tourism
w english.visitbeijing.com

Bespoke Travel Company
w bespoketravelcompany.com

China Highlights
w chinahighlights.com

Discover Beijing Tours
w discoverbeijingtours.com

Travel China Guide
w travelchinaguide.com

Places to Stay

PRICE CATEGORIES

Prices are based on a double room per night (with breakfast if included), with taxes and extra charges.

¥ under ¥400, ¥¥ ¥400–¥1,400, ¥¥¥ over ¥1,400

Luxury and Boutique Hotels

Brickyard

MAP H5 ▪ Beigou Village, near Mutianyu, Great Wall, Huairou ▪ 6162 6506 ▪ www.brickyard atmutianyu.com ▪ ¥¥

Beijing expats' first choice for romantic getaways, girls' weekends, and even weddings, the Brickyard features some impressive floor-to-ceiling windows, utterly breathtaking views, and beautiful gardens. Enjoy excellent meals made from locally sourced ingredients, and bring your swimsuit to take full advantage of the popular outdoor Jacuzzi.

New World Beijing

MAP F5 ▪ 8 Qinian Jie ▪ 5960 8888 ▪ Subway: Chongwenmen ▪ www. beijing.newworldhotels. com ▪ ¥¥

Well-located between the Temple of Heaven and Wangfujing, this hotel offers comfortable and smart rooms, a Jacuzzi and a swimming pool. It also has two Chinese restaurants, a tearoom, and a rooftop bar.

Mandarin Oriental

MAP M4 ▪ 269 Wangfujing Dajie, Dongcheng District ▪ 8509 8888 ▪ www. mandarinoriental.com ▪ ¥¥¥

Beijing's first Mandarin Oriental has palatial suites with Forbidden City views, a central Wangfujing location, and a terrace cocktail bar and posh steakhouse. This is one of the best luxury hotels in Beijing.

Shadow Art Puppet Hotel

MAP D2 ▪ 24 Songshu Street, Xicheng District ▪ 8328 7847 ▪ www. shadowartboutique.com ▪ ¥¥

In addition to three weekly puppet shows, this themed hotel in historic Shichaihai also offers some free calligraphy, puppet-painting and dumpling-making classes, plus free access to bikes. Hou Hai is only minutes away.

Aman at the Summer Palace

MAP G6 ▪ 1 Gong Men Qian Jie ▪ 5987 9999 ▪ www.amanresorts.com ▪ ¥¥¥

Guests at this stunning hotel 6 miles (10 km) northwest of the city center enjoy private access to the Summer Palace (see pp28–9), as well as a cinema, stylish spa, and subterranean swimming pool.

China World Summit Wing

MAP H4 ▪ 1 Jianguo Men Wai Dajie ▪ 6505 2299 ▪ Subway: Guomao ▪ www.shangri-la.com/ beijing ▪ ¥¥¥

This hotel in Beijing's second-tallest tower affords stunning city views from its swish Atmosphere bar on the 80th floor. There are also four restaurants, a spa, and an infinity pool.

Eclat Beijing

MAP H3 ▪ 9 Dongdaqiao Lu, Chaoyang District ▪ 8561 2888 ▪ www.eclat hotels.com/beijing ▪ ¥¥¥

A stylishly designed boutique hotel with an impressive art collection in the public spaces, Eclat Beijing also has the capital's first pool suites. It offers a 24-hour food lounge, plus other facilities such as a personal butler service.

Hotel Côte Cour

MAP F3 ▪ 70 Yanyue Hutong ▪ 6523 9598 ▪ Subway: Dongsi ▪ www. hotelcotecourbj.com ▪ ¥¥¥

Hidden away amid a maze of local *hutongs*, this comfortable boutique hotel presents a modern take on a traditional *siheyuan* courtyard house. It has stylish fittings and under-floor heating that is very welcome in winter.

NUO Hotel

MAP H6 ▪ 2 Jiangtai Road, Chaoyang District ▪ 5926 8888 ▪ www. nuohotel.com ▪ ¥¥¥

China's groundbreaking foray into the luxury market, NUO is the first among a planned group of 15 hotels in various global capitals. Contemporary art superstar Zeng Fanzhi, who served as a consultant, installed his own original art, building a theme for the hotel's 798 Art District location.

The Opposite House
MAP H2 ■ 11 Sanlitun Road ■ 6417 6688 ■ Subway: Tuanjiehu ■ www.theopposite house.com ■ ¥¥¥

Designed by renowned Japanese architect Kengo Kuma, The Opposite House is part of Taikoo Li Sanlitun. The 99 spacious rooms, all with natural wooden floors and deep oak soaking tubs, are a design experience, as is the stainless-steel pool.

Park Hyatt Beijing
MAP H4 ■ 2 Jianguo Men Dajie ■ 8567 1234 ■ Subway: Guomao ■ www.hyatt.com ■ ¥¥¥

High-end service and style are the watchwords at the Park Hyatt hotel. Chic, contemporary accommodations, coupled with stylish bars and restaurants, draw the most discerning of local and international clients.

The Peninsula Beijing
MAP N4 ■ 8 Jinyu Hutong ■ 8516 2888 ■ Subway: Dengshikou ■ www.peninsula.com ■ ¥¥¥

Converted to an all-suite hotel in 2017, with every luxury imaginable. Two upscale restaurants (Huang Ting and Jing), excellent service, and a central location make this one of the city's best accommodation choices.

Waldorf Astoria Beijing
MAP N4 ■ 5-15 Jinyu Hutong, off Wangfujing Street, Dongcheng District ■ 8520 8989 ■ www.waldorfastoria3. hilton.com ■ ¥¥¥

This is the jewel of downtown Beijing.

Guests rave about the creative design, contemporary art display, prime location, and excellent service. For an ultra luxurious China experience, book the premium Hutong Villa, which features a private swimming pool.

Courtyard Hotels

Red Lantern House
MAP D2 ■ 5 Zheng Jue Hutong, Xinjiekou Nan Dajie, Xicheng ■ 8328 3935 ■ Subway: Jishuitan ■ ¥

The family-owned Red Lantern House occupies a main building and two pretty courtyards. It is only a stone's throw away from the lively bars of Hou Hai.

Bamboo Garden Hotel
MAP E1 ■ 24 Xiao Shi Qiao Hutong ■ 5852 0088 ■ Subway: Gulou Dajie ■ www.bbgh.com. cn ■ ¥¥

Close to Hou Hai lake, this is the oldest of Beijing's traditional hotels, with the largest and probably most elaborate courtyards, plus beautiful rockeries and covered pathways.

Double Happiness
MAP E2 ■ 37 Dongsisitiao, Dongcheng District ■ 6400 7762 ■ Subway: Dongsi ■ www.double happinesscourtyard hotel.com ■ ¥¥

A hotel with a great ambience, Double Happiness has small rooms with traditional decor but modern bathrooms. There are lovely little courtyards outside the rooms along with a pleasant patio.

161 Lama Temple Courtyard Hotel
MAP F2 ■ 46 Beixinqiao Santiao Hutong ■ 8401 5027 ■ Subway: Beixinqiao ■ ¥¥

A well-run hotel, part of a small chain of courtyard properties, 161 Lama Temple Courtyard Hotel has around a dozen compact but comfortable rooms. It is set in a great location between the Lama Temple and the restaurants of Gui Jie (Ghost Street).

Fly by Knight Courtyard
MAP F3 ■ 6 Dengcao Hutong, Dongcheng ■ 6559 7966 ■ www. flybyknightbeijing.com ■ ¥¥

One of the best-value *hutong* guesthouses, this friendly, clean and well run ex-hostel has spacious and comfortable traditional rooms, as well as an excellent English-speaking staff. The kung fu classes organized in the hotel courtyard are a bonus.

Kelly's Courtyard
MAP C3 ■ 25 Xiaoyuan Hutong, off Bingmasi Hutong, Xisi South Street ■ 6611 8515 ■ Subway: Xisi ■ Bus: 47, 105, 690, or 808 ■ www.kellyscourtyard. com ■ ¥¥

A stylish and modernized hideaway in a historic *hutong* near Xidan and the financial district, this hostel is owned by a travel-loving Chinese fashion designer.

The Orchid

MAP E2 ▪ 65 Baochao Hutong, Dongcheng District ▪ 8565 9295 ▪ ¥¥

Tucked away down a quiet *hutong* in the hippest, chicest part of Beijing's Old City, The Orchid features whitewashed, airy rooms with polished hardwood floors, plus an excellent breakfast. The atmospheric terrace restaurant offers a range of Chinese, South Asian, as well as Middle Eastern meals, and serves sundowners all day long.

Business Hotels

East

22 Jiuxianqiao Rd, Chaoyang ▪ 8426 0888 ▪ www.east-beijing.com ▪ ¥¥

Set amid parkland in the INDIGO business district, this contemporary hotel caters to the high-end business traveler. All 369 rooms and 23 executive suites have amenities including an LCD TV, free Wi-Fi, Bose audio system and rainfall showers in the bathroom. The hotel also has two good restaurants, a swimming pool, and gym facilities.

Park Plaza Hotel

MAP N3 ▪ 97 Jinbao Jie ▪ 8522 1999 ▪ Subway: Wangfujing ▪ www. parkplaza.com/ beijingcn ▪ ¥¥

The stylish Park Plaza is a peaceful oasis close to the shops and sights of Wangfujing. Guest rooms feature stylish designer touches, and the hotel is conveniently located for both the Forbidden City and Tian'an Men Square.

Four Seasons Beijing

MAP H1 ▪ 48 Liang Ma Qiao Lu ▪ 5695 8888 ▪ www.fourseasons.com/ beijing ▪ ¥¥¥

Exemplary service and premium amenities await business and leisure travelers who stay at this impressive modern hotel. The interiors are artistic, and the hotel also has two signature restaurants, a deluxe spa, and a popular lounge bar.

Hilton Beijing Wangfujing

MAP M4 ▪ 8 Wangfujing Dong Dajie ▪ 5812 8888 ▪ Subway: Wangfujing ▪ www.hilton.com ▪ ¥¥¥

Spacious, open-plan rooms, warm service, and a large swimming pool are just some of the draws at this hotel. A central location within walking distance of Tian'an Men Square and the Forbidden City is another key feature.

Kerry Center Hotel

MAP H4 ▪ 1 Guanghua Lu ▪ 6561 8833 ▪ Subway: Guomao ▪ www.shangri-la.com ▪ ¥¥¥

The Kerry Center Hotel combines the Shangri-La group's high service standards with bright, modern room design. The Kerry is also home to the Centro cocktail bar *(see p59)* and extensive health facilities.

Cordis Beijing Capital Airport

MAP H5 ▪ 1 Yi Jing Rd, opposite Terminal 3 ▪ 6457 5555 ▪ Subway: Beijing International Airport ▪ www.cordis hotels.com ▪ ¥¥

Located near Beijing Capital Airport, this hotel offers luxury rooms and suites, as well as several modern restaurants and bars, a club lounge, gym, free Wi-Fi and an art gallery. There is also a free airport shuttle bus service.

The Ritz-Carlton, Beijing

MAP H6 ▪ 83A Jianguo Lu, China Central Place, Chaoyang District ▪ 5908 8888 ▪ Subway: Dawanglu ▪ www. ritzcarlton.com ▪ ¥¥¥

A perfect retreat for both business and leisure travelers, this 305-room deluxe hotel offers fine dining, excellent facilities for meetings and events, and a high-end spa.

The Westin Beijing Chaoyang

MAP H1 ▪ Bei San Huan Dajie ▪ 5922 8888 ▪ Subway: Liangma Qiao ▪ www.marriott. com ▪ ¥¥¥

Outstanding service is complemented by stylish decor here. Being set on a ring road is not ideal, but the main sights and shopping areas are only a short taxi ride away.

Mid-Range Hotels

Red Hotel

MAP G2 ▪ 10 Taiping Zhuang Chunxiu Lu ▪ 6417 1066 ▪ Subway: Dong Zhi Men ▪ www. red-hotel.com ▪ ¥

Staying true to its name, the former Red House Hotel stands out with its vibrant facade. This establishment offers clean, cheerful rooms, which are good value for money. There's a popular soccer bar on the premises, and it's a short walk to more bars in the Sanlitun District.

Crystal Orange

MAP G4 ■ 25 Yonganli Zhong Jie, Chaoyang ■ 6566 1515 ■ Subway: Yonganli ■ ¥¥

This good-value hotel chain is furnished in bold colors, with Andy Warhol prints adorning the walls of the lobby. Comfortable rooms have spacious bathrooms and feature all modern conveniences, including Wi-Fi and iPod docks.

Grand Mercure Dongcheng

MAP N6 ■ 101 Jiaodaokou Dongdajie ■ 8403 1188 ■ Subway: Beixinqiao ■ ¥¥

A comfortable and highly affordable chain hotel, Grand Mercure Dongcheng is located just a short walk from the *hutongs* of Gulou. It offers modern, business-like rooms that come equipped with modern amenities. Opt for the executive floor for free evening drinks.

Holiday Inn Express Dong Zhi Men

MAP G2 ■ 1 Chunxiu Lu, Dongcheng ■ 6416 9999 ■ Subway: Dong Zhi Men ■ www.hi express.com ■ ¥¥

Centrally located between Dong Zhi Men and Gongti Bei Lu, with easy access to the city's main attractions, Holiday Inn Express offers rooms at affordable prices. A good breakfast is included in the room rate, as is Wi-Fi.

Ibis Dongdaqiao

MAP N4 ■ 30 Zhongfang Jie, Nansanlitun Lu ■ 6508 8100 ■ Subway: Dongdaqiao ■ ¥¥

This no-frills chain hotel is dependable and set on a leafy street within walking distance of the bright lights of Sanlitun. Be sure to ask for a room with a window.

Penta Beijing

MAP F5 ■ 3–18 Chongwen Men Wai Daije, Dongcheng ■ 6708 1188 ■ Subway: Beijing Railway Station ■ www.pentahotels. com ■ ¥¥

Located close to Tian'an Men Square and the Temple of Heaven, this stylish hotel is suited to those traveling for business and leisure. As well as good and modern in-room facilities, it offers a lounge, gym, games area, and free Wi-Fi.

Budget Hotels

Beijing Drum Tower Youth Hostel

MAP E2 ■ 51 Jiugulou Dajie ■ 8401 6565 ■ Subway: Gulou Dajie ■ ¥

Japanese capsule-style singles, as well as shared dorms, are on offer at this budget hostel on the edge of a buzzy *hutong* district. Modern amenities and simple rooms make this a comfortable stay.

Leo Hostel

MAP L6 ■ 52 Dazhalan Xijie ■ 6303 0879 ■ Subway: Qian Men ■ www.leohostel.com ■ ¥

Leo Hostel benefits from an excellent location south of Tian'an Men Square, in among old lanes. Rooms range from four to ten-bed dorms to doubles. Facilities include free Wi-Fi, computer with internet connection, a pool table and a second-hand book exchange.

365 Inn

MAP L6 ■ 55 Dashilan Xijie ■ 6308 5956 ■ Subway: Dengshikou ■ ¥

Situated on a busy street close to Tian'an Men Square, 365 Inn has dorms and doubles, and a lively bar-restaurant where guests drink inexpensive Tsingtao beer and catch up on the day's adventures.

Peking Station Hostel

MAP F4 ■ 12 Babaolou Hutong ■ Subway: Beijing Railway Station ■ ¥

A plant-filled oasis in a *hutong* close to Beijing's main train station, this petite, immaculately kept hostel is a great option for solo travelers and those valuing peace and quiet.

The Peking International Youth Hostel

MAP E2 ■ 113-2 Nan Luogu Xiang, Dongcheng District ■ 6401 3961/ 8403 9098 ■ ¥¥

Owned by a local flower designer, this popular hostel exudes shabby-chic decor and has an outdoor courtyard – the latter, a rare budget treat. The restaurant, while comparatively pricey, rates high, and helpful staff will arrange show tickets and day trips for you. The bustling local neighborhood is a favorite with Beijingers.

General Index

Acknowledgments

This edition updated by

Contributor Thomas O'Malley
Senior Editor Alison McGill
Senior Designer Stuti Tiwari
Project Editors Dipika Dasgupta, Rada Radojicic
Editor Nayan Keshan
Picture Research Administrator Vagisha Pushp
Publishing Assistant Halima Mohammed
Jacket Designer Jordan Lambley
Senior Cartographer Mohammad Hassan
Cartography Manager Suresh Kumar
DTP Designer Rohit Rojal
Senior Production Editor Jason Little
Production Controller Kariss Ainsworth
Deputy Managing Editor Beverly Smart
Managing Editors Shikha Kulkarni, Hollie Teague
Managing Art Editor Sarah Snelling
Senior Managing Art Editor Priyanka Thakur
Art Director Maxine Pedliham
Publishing Director Georgina Dee

DK would like to thank the following for their contribution to the previous editions: Andrew Humphreys, Helen Peters, David Leffman, Chen Chao.
The publisher would like to thank the following for their kind permission to reproduce their photographs:
Key: a-above; b-below/bottom; c-centre; f-far; l-left; r-right; t-top

123RF.com: Brian Kinney 4t, 16-7.

4Corners: Günter Gräfenhain 4cra; HP Huber 17cr; SIME / Tull & Bruno Morandi 35bl.

Alamy Stock Photo: age fotostock 14cla; / Yuen Man Cheung 30-1c; avadaRM 17crb; Sergio Azenha 53cl; Blue Jean Images 49cr, 52tl; Jon Bower China 11bl; Robert Burch 89tl; China Images 27bl; EPA 18cl; epa european pressphoto agency b.v. 46cl, 65br; Dmitry Erokhin 69tr; F1online digitale Bildagentur GmbH 96c; Wayne Farrell 64c; Kevin Foy 90cl; Victor Fraile 44cl; Jan Fritz 29tl; David Gee 3 15tc; Manfred Gottschalk 62c; 70cla; Tim Graham 33tr; Hemis 53tr, 90-1; Henry Westheim Photography 4clb, 33bl; jeremy sutton-hibbert 105tl; Kate Hockenhull 83tl; Iconotec 91cl; imageBROKER 71cl, 104br; jejim120 12br; JLImages 65clb; John Warburton-Lee Photography 26cla, 105cr; Patric Jonsson 82b; kpzfoto 81tr; Keith Levit 61b; Sean Pavone 2tl, 3tl, 8-9, 66-7, 86-7; Wiliam Perry 76tr; Prisma Bildagentur AG 82c; Dirk Renckhoff 11tc, 54cl; REUTERS 64t, 75br; robertharding 46b; RosalreneBetancourt 10 73cl; Hans-Joachim Schneider 39tr; Felix Stensson 99br; Keren Su / China Span 34clb; SuperStock 92cla; Ulana Switucha 27tl; TAO Images Limited 32cl, 43bl, 52c, 94tl, / Ren Shulin 30br, Lucas Vallecillos 32-3c; Lucas Vallecillos 25tc; Steve Vidler 12cl, 15cl, 60tl; View Stock 51br; Viewstock 41t; John Woods 11cl; Xinhua 51cl.

AWL Images: Christian Kober 3tr, 106-7; Travel Pix Collection 28bl.

Cafe Zarah: 84tl.

Cai Yi Xuan: Ken Seet 57bl.

Courtesy Ullens Center for Contemporary Art: 31cr.

Dreamstime.com: 06photo 10ca; Aakahunaa 40c; Kyle Allen 13tl; Leonid Andronov 13br, 80ca; Beijing Hetuchuangyi Images Co. Ltd. 46tc; Bertrandb 68clb; Caoerlei 34-5; Chinaview 54tr; Chucky 78c; Chuyu 95br; Cowardlion 25cr; Dk88888 10crb; 63br; Julie Feinstein 58bl; Fotokon 21tl, 57tr; Frenta 98c; Igor Groshev 35cr; Hungchungchih 7tr; Icara 11cra; Attila Jandi 74cl; Mike K 63tl; Klodien 102tl; Leonidfeng 70b; Peng Li 79b; Yong hian Lim 76b; Linqong 45tr; Luoxubin 45bl; Mengtianhan 2tr, 36-7; Miragik 55cl; Angela Ostafichuk 100t; Sean Pavone 4b,18-9; William Perry 99tl; Ppy2010ha 54bl; Qin0377 10cl; Mario Savoia 55br; Yanhui Song 95t; Sutsaiy 85bc; Libo Tang 50t; Telnyawka 21cr; Winghoong Thong 4cla; Tiffanychan 44t; Tktktk 72b; Vincentstthomas 21br; Vitalyedush 7bl, 10bl, 19br, 20-1, 40tl; Zheng Xiaoqiao 103br; Yuri Yavnik 103t; Xi Zhang 4cl, 75tl; Zhaohui 52b; Zhiwei Zhou 22-3; Vladimir Zhuravlev 10cr; Zjm7100 27cr, 48tl, 61tl, 68tl, 101cl.

The Georg: 56clb.

Getty Images: AFP / STR 64br; Beijing Youth Daily / Visual China Group 30clb; China Photos 48b; De Agostini / W. Buss 28-9; DEA Picture Library 38b; DuKai photographer 88tl; Manfred Gottschalk 78tl; Hulton Fine Art Collection 38tc; Gamma-Keystone 39cl; Christian Kober 100clb; Keith Levit 50bl; Luis Castaneda Inc. 4crb, 16bl, 96t; Tuul and Bruno Morandi 11crb; MyLoupe 20clb; Paris Match Archive 15br; Shi Shuai / Costfoto / Future Publishing 49tl; Sino Images 29cr; Paul Souders 42clb; South China Morning Post / Simon Song 58t, 59clb; Travelasia 43b, 61cr; Wang Yukun / Moment 14b, 99tl.

iStockphoto.com: aphotostory 12-3, 62b; bpperry 81tr; fotoVoyager 6cl; hxdyl 1; loonger 104t; rabbit75_ist 25clb; Siegfried Schnepf 24bl; VitalyEdush 18br; willcao911 41tl; zhaojiankang 24-5.

Jianghu Bar: 59br.

Mosto: 56t.

Robert Harding Picture Library: Directphoto 26-7.

Shutterstock.com: cowardlion 43crb; Wirestock Creators 89b.

SuperStock: Dirk Renckhoff / imageBROKER 47tl.

The Taco Bar: 93clb.

Cover
Front and spine: **iStockphoto.com:** hxdyl.

Back: **iStockphoto.com:** hxdyl b; **Dreamstime. com:** Sean Pavone tr, Yulan tl; **iStockphoto. com:** ispyfriend crb, Yestock cla.

Pull Out Map Cover
iStockphoto.com: hxdyl.

All other images © Dorling Kindersley
For further information see:
www.dkimages.com

Penguin
Random
House

First edition 2007

Published in Great Britain by
Dorling Kindersley Limited
DK, One Embassy Gardens, 8 Viaduct
Gardens, London SW11 7BW, UK

The authorised representative in the EEA is
Dorling Kindersley Verlag GmbH. Arnulfstr.
124, 80636 Munich, Germany

Published in the United States by
DK Publishing, 1745 Broadway, 20th Floor,
New York, NY 10019, USA

A CIP catalog record is available
from the British Library.

A catalog record for this book is available
from the Library of Congress.

ISSN 1479-344X
ISBN 978 0 2415 6896 5

Printed and bound in Malaysia.

www.dk.com

*As a guide to abbreviations in visitor information
blocks:* **Adm** = admission charge; **D** = dinner.

MIX
Paper | Supporting
responsible forestry
FSC www.fsc.org **FSC™ C018179**

This book was made with Forest
Stewardship Council™ certified
paper – one small step in DK's
commitment to a sustainable future.
**For more information go to
www.dk.com/our-green-pledge**

Phrase Book

The Chinese language belongs to the Sino-Tibetan family of languages and uses characters which are ideographic – a symbol is used to represent an idea or an object. Mandarin Chinese, known as Putonghua in mainland China, is fairly straightforward as each character is monosyllabic. Traditionally, Chinese is written in vertical columns from top right to bottom left, however the Western style is widely used. There are several Romanization systems; the Pinyin system used here is the official system in mainland China. This phrase book gives the English word or phrase, followed by the Chinese script, then the Pinyin.

Guidelines

Pronounce vowels as in these English words:

a = as in "father"

e = as in "lurch"

i = as in "see"

o = as in "solid"

u = as in "pooh"

ü = as the French u or German ü (place your lips to say "oo" and try to say "ee")

Letter combinations

Most of the consonants are pronounced as in English. As a rough guide, pronounce the following consonants as in these English words:

c = as ts in "hats"

q = as ch in "cheat"

x = as sh in "sheet"

z = as ds in "heads"

zh = as j in "Joe"

Mandarin Chinese is a tonal language with four tones, represented in Pinyin by one of the following marks above each vowel – the symbol shows whether the tone is flat, rising, falling and rising, or falling. The Chinese characters do not convey this information: tones are learnt when the character is learnt. Teaching tones is beyond the scope of this small phrase book, but a language course book with a CD or app will help those who wish to take the language farther.

Dialects

There are many Chinese dialects in use. It is hard to guess exactly how many, but they can be roughly classified into one of seven large groups (Mandarin, Cantonese, Hakka, Hui, etc.), each group containing a large number of more minor dialects. Although all these dialects are quite different – Cantonese uses six tones instead of four – Mandarin or Putonghua, which is mainly based on the Beijing dialect, is the official language. Despite these differences all Chinese people are more or less able to use the same formal written language so they can understand each other's writing, if not each other's speech.

In an Emergency

Help!	请帮忙！	Qing bangmang
Stop!	停住	Ting zhu
Call a doctor!	叫医生！	Jiao yisheng
Call an ambulance!	叫救护车！	Jiao jiuhuche
Call the police!	叫警察！	Jiao jiingcha
Fire!	火！	Huo
Where is the hospital/police station?	医院/警察分局在哪里?	Yiyuan/jingcha fenju zai nali?

Communication Essentials

Hello	你好	Nihao
Goodbye	再见	Zaijian
Yes/No	是 / 不是	Shi/Bushi
… not …	不 …	bushi
I'm from…	我是 … 人	Wo shi … ren
I understand	我明白	Wo mingbai
I don't know	我不知道	Wo bu zhidao
Thank you	谢谢你	Xiexie ni
Thank you very much	多谢	Duo xie
Thanks (casual)	谢谢	Xiexie
You're welcome	不用谢	Bu yong xie
No, thank you	不，谢谢你	Bu, xiexie ni
Please (offering)	请	Qing
Please (asking)	请问	Qing wen
I don't understand	我不明白	Wo Bu mingbai
Sorry/Excuse me!	抱歉 / 对不起	Baoqian/ Duibuqi
Could you help me please? (not emergency)	你能帮助我吗?	Ni neng bang zhu wo ma?

Useful Phrases

My name is ….	我叫 …	Wo jiao …
Goodbye	再见	Zaijian
What is (this)?	（这）是什么?	(zhe) shi shenme?
Could I possibly have …? (very polite)	能不能请你给我 …?	Neng buneng qing ni gei wo …?
Is there … here?	这儿有 … 吗?	Zhe'r you … ma?
Where can I get …?	我在哪里可以得到 …?	Wo zai na li keyi de dao …?
How much is it?	它要多少钱?	Ta yao duoshao qian?
What time is …?	… 什么时间?	… shenme shijian?
Cheers! (toast)	干杯!	Ganbei!
Where is the restroom/toilet?	卫生间 / 洗手间在哪里?	Weishengjian/ Xishoujian zai nali?

Signs

open	开	kai
closed	关	guan
entrance	入口	renkou
exit	出口	chukou
danger	危险	weixian
emergency exit	安全门	anquanmen
information	信息	xinxi
restroom	卫生间	Weishengjian/
toilet	洗手间	Xishoujian
men	男士	nanshi
women	女士	nüshi

Money

bank	银行	yinhang
cash	现金	xianjin
credit card	信用卡	xinyongka
currency exchange office	外汇兑换处	waihui duihuanchu
dollars	美元	meiyuan
pounds	英镑	yingbang
yuan	元	yuan

Keeping in Touch

Where is a telephone?	电话在哪里?	*Dianhua zai nali?*
May I use your phone?	我可以用你的电话吗?	*Wo keyi yong nide dianhua ma?*
cell phone	手机	*shouji*
sim card	卡	*sim ka*
Hello, this is ...	你好，我是 ...	*Nihao, wo shi...*
airmail	航空	*hangkong*
email	电子邮件	*dianzi youjian*
fax	传真	*chuanzhen*
Internet	互联网	*hulianwang*
postcard	明信片	*mingxinpian*
post office	邮局	*youju*
stamp	邮票	*youpiao*
telephone card	电话卡	*dianhua ka*

Shopping

Where can I buy ...?	我可以在哪里买到 ...?	*Wo keyi zai nali maidao ...?*
How much *does this cost?*	这要多少钱?	*Zhe yao duoshao qian?*
Too expensive!	太贵了!	*Tai gui le!*
Do you have ...?	你有 ... 吗?	*Ni you ... ma?*
May I try this on?	我可以试穿吗?	*Wo keyi shi chuan ma?*
Please show me that.	请给我看看那个。	*Qing gei wo kankan na ge.*

Sightseeing

Where is ...?	... 在哪里?	*... zai nali?*
How do I get to ...?	我怎么到 ...?	*Wo zenme dao ...?*
Is it far?	远不远?	*Yuan bu yuan?*
bridge	桥	*qiao*
city	城市	*chengshi*
city center	市中心	*shi zhongxin*
gardens	花园	*huayuan*
mountain	山	*shan*
museum	博物馆	*bowuguan*
palace	宫殿	*gongdian*
park	公园	*gongyuan*
port	港口	*gangkou*
river	江，河	*jiang, he*
ruins	废墟	*feixu*
shopping area	购物区	*gouwu qu*
shrine	神殿	*shendian*
street	街	*jie*
temple	寺 / 庙	*si/miao*
town	镇	*zhen*
village	村	*cun*
zoo	动物园	*dongwuyuan*
north	北	*bei*
south	南	*nan*
east	东	*dong*
west	西	*xi*
left/right	左 / 右	*zuo/you*
straight ahead	一直向前	*yizhi xiangqian*

Getting Around

airport	机场	*jichang*
bicycle	自行车	*zixingche*
I want to rent a bicycle.	我想租一辆自行车。	*Wo xiang zu yiliang zixingche.*

ordinary bus	公共汽车	*gonggong qiche*
express bus	特快公共汽车	*tekuai gonggong qiche*
minibus	面包车	*mianbaoche*
main bus station	公共汽车总站	*gonggong qiche zong zhan*
Which bus goes to ...?	哪一路公共汽车到 ... 去?	*Nayilu gonggong qiche dao ... qu?*
Please tell me where to get off.	请告诉我在哪里下车。	*Qing gaosu wo zai nali xia che.*
car	小汽车	*xiaoqiche*
ferry	渡船	*duchuan*
baggage room	行李室	*xingli shi*
one-way ticket	单程票	*dancheng piao*
return ticket	往返票	*wangfan piao*
taxi	出租车	*chuzuche*
ticket	票	*piao*
ticket office	售票处	*shoupiao chu*
timetable	时刻表	*shikebiao*

Accommodations

air-conditioning	空调	*kongtiao*
bath	洗澡	*xizao*
check out	退房	*tui fang*
deposit	定金	*dingjin*
double bed	双人床	*shuangren chuang*
hair dryer	吹风机	*chuifeng ji*
room	房间	*fangjian*
economy room	经济房	*jingji fang*
key	钥匙	*yaoshi*
front desk	前台	*qiantai*
single/ twin room	单人 / 双人房	*danren/ shuangren fang*
single beds	单人床	*danren chuang*
shower	淋浴	*linyu*
standard room	标准房间	*biaozhun fangjian*
deluxe suite	豪华套房	*haohua taofang*

Eating Out

May I see the menu?	请给我看看菜单。	*Qing gei wo kankan caidan?*
Is there a set menu?	有没有套餐?	*You meiyou taocan?*
I'd like	我想要 ...	*Wo xiang yao...*
May I have one of those?	请给我这个。	*Qing gei wo zhege?*
I am a vegetarian.	我是素食者。	*Wo shi sushizhe.*
Waiter/Waitress!	服务员!	*Fuwuyuan!*
May I have a fork/knife/ spoon	请给我一把叉 / 刀 / 汤匙。	*Qing gei wo yiba cha/dao/ tangshi*
May we have the check please.	请把帐单开给我们。	*Qing ba zhangdan kaigei women.*
breakfast	早餐	*zaocan*
buffet	自助餐	*zizhucan*
chopsticks	筷子	*kuaizi*
dinner	晚餐	*wancan*
to drink	喝	*he*

to eat	吃	chi
food	食品	shipin
full (stomach)	饱	bao
hot/cold	热 / 冷	re/leng
hungry	饿	e
lunch	午餐	wucan
set menu	套餐	taocan
spicy	酸辣	suan la
hot (spicy)	辣	la
sweet	甜	tian
mild	淡	dan
Western food	西餐	xi can
restaurant	餐馆	canguan
restaurant (upscale)	饭店	fandian

Food

apple	苹果	pingguo
bacon	咸肉	xianrou
bamboo shoots	笋	sun
beancurd	豆腐	doufu
bean sprouts	豆芽	dou ya
beans	豆	dou
beef	牛肉	niurou
bread	面包	mianbao
butter	黄油	huangyou
chicken	鸡	ji
crab	蟹	xie
duck	鸭	ya
eel	鳗	man
egg	蛋	dan
eggplant	茄子	qiezi
fermented soybean paste	酱	jiang
fish	鱼	yu
fried egg	炒蛋	chao dan
fried tofu	油豆腐	you doufu
fruit	水果	shuiguo
ginger	姜	jiang
ice cream	冰淇淋	bingqilin
meat	肉	rou
melon	瓜	gua
noodles	面	mian
egg noodles	鸡蛋面	jidan mian
wheat flour noodles	面粉面	mianfen mian
rice flour noodles	米粉面	mifen mian
omelet	煎蛋饼	jiandanbing
onion	洋葱	yangcong
peach	桃子	taozi
pepper	胡椒粉, 辣椒	hujiaofen, lajiao
pickles	泡菜	paocai
pork	猪肉	zhurou
potato	土豆	tudou
rice	米饭	mifan
rice crackers	爆米花饼	baomihua bing'gan
salad	色拉	sala
salmon	鲑鱼, 大马哈鱼	guiyu, damahayu

salt	盐	yan
scallion	韭葱	jiucong
seaweed	海带	haidai
shrimp	虾	xia
soup	汤	tang
soy sauce	酱油	jiangyou
squid	鱿鱼	youyu
steak	牛排	niupai
sugar	糖	tang
vegetables	蔬菜	shucai
yoghurt	酸奶	suannai

Drinks

beer	啤酒	pijiu
black tea	红茶	hong cha
coffee (hot)	(热) 咖啡	(re) kafei
fruit juice	果汁	guo zhi
rice wine	米酒	mi jiu
green tea	绿茶	lü cha
iced coffee	冰咖啡	bing kafei
milk	牛奶	niunai
mineral water	矿泉水	kuang quanshui
orange juice	橙汁	cheng zhi
wine	葡萄酒	putaojiu

Numbers

0	零	ling
1	一	yi
2	二	er
3	三	san
4	四	si
5	五	wu
6	六	liu
7	七	qi
8	八	ba
9	九	jiu
10	十	shi
11	十一	shiyi
12	十二	shier
20	二十	ershi
21	二十一	ershi yi
22	二十二	ershi er
30	三十	sanshi
40	四十	sishi
100	一百	yi bai
101	一百零一	yi bai ling yi
200	二百	er bai

Time

Monday	星期一	xingqiyi
Tuesday	星期二	xingqi'er
Wednesday	星期三	xingqisan
Thursday	星期四	xingqisi
Friday	星期五	xingqiwu
Saturday	星期六	xingqiliu
Sunday	星期天	xingqitian
today	今天	jintian
yesterday	昨天	zuotian
tomorrow	明天	mingtian